A Love Letter to the Ladies:
A Single Christian Man's Perspective

Estanislao (T.J.) Hurtado III

Estanislao (T.J.) Hurtado III
Fiesta Publishing
Phoenix, Arizona

A Love Letter to the Ladies: A Single Christian Man's Perspective

Copyright © 2018 by Estanislao (T.J.) Hurtado III

All rights reserved. No part of this book may be reproduced in any written, electronic, recording, or photocopying form without written permission of the publisher.

ISBN: 978-0-9643613-9-3

10 9 8 7 6 5 4 3 2 1

Printed in the United States of America

Library of Congress Control Number: 2018930959

Unless otherwise identified all scripture quotations are taken from the New American Standard Bible®, © 1960, 1962, 1963, 1968, 1971, 1972, 1973, 1975, 1977, 1995 by The Lockman Foundation. Used with permission. (Lockman.org)

Scripture quotations marked NIV® are taken from the Holy Bible, New International Version ®. Copyright © 1973, 1978, 1984, 2011 by Biblica, Inc. ®. Used with permission. All rights reserved worldwide.

Scripture taken from the New King James Version®. © 1982 by Thomas Nelson. Used with permission. All rights reserved.

Scripture quotations marked ASV are from the American Standard Bible. Copyright © 1960, 1962, 1968, 1971, 1972, 1973, 1975, by the Lockman Foundation. Used by permission. All rights reserved.

Scripture quotations marked NLT are from the Holy Bible, New Living Translation. Copyright © 1996.Used by permission of Tyndale House Publishers, Inc., Wheaton, Illinois 60189. All rights reserved.

Scripture quotations marked by AMP are from the Amplified Bible. Old Testament copyright © 1965, 1987 by the Zondervan Corporation. The Amplified New Testament. Copyright © 1954, 1958, 1987 by the Lockman Foundation. Used by permission.

Scripture quotations marked by The Message are from The Message. Copyright © by Eugene H. Peterson, 1993, 1994, 1995. Used by permission of NavPress Publishing Group.

Scripture quotations marked by Complete Jewish Bible are from the Complete Jewish Bible. Copyright © by David H. Stern 1998. Used by permission of Jewish New Testament Publications, Inc. All rights reserved.

Scripture quotations marked KJV are from the King James Version of the Bible.

Most names have been changed in an effort to protect the privacy and/or ensure the safety of individuals included in this book.

Cover and Interior Design by: Sebastian Herran

Fiesta Publishing
fiestapublishing.com

Dedication

To my loving sister Tina, who went to be with the Lord July 7, 2016; to my spiritual mother Marilyn, who went to be with the Lord February 14, 2018, and to the ladies who are seeking the Lord's unconditional love and wisdom in order to be blessed with their future husband.

Table of Contents

Introduction i

Chapter 1: The Price of Purity *1*

Chapter 2: Turn Your Pain into Power *15*

Chapter 3: My Personal Story of Pain *27*

Chapter 4: Eternal Intimacy Brings True Harmony *41*

Chapter 5: Whom Are You Trying to Attract? *59*

Chapter 6: It Starts with the Heart *77*

Chapter 7: Know Your True Identity *105*

Chapter 8: Marriage – Your Future Hope *127*

    Acknowledgments *141*

    Notes *145*

A Love Letter to the Ladies

Introduction

This is your beginning. Your Father knows what is best for you from before you were born to the day your spirit leaves this earth, and every moment and experience in between. The intent for this book comes from an absolute passion to see you, my dear sister, and all of my sisters in the Lord, fulfill what Jesus called the greatest commandment:

> *"You are to love ADONAI your God with all your heart and with all your soul and with all your strength." This is the greatest and most important mitzvah. And a second is similar to it, "You are to love your neighbor as yourself." All of the Torah and the Prophets are dependent on these two mitzvot.*
>
> Matthew 22:37-40 (Complete Jewish Bible)

Let me clarify the meaning of a few words. *Mitzvah* and *mitzvot*, as they are used in the above scripture in the Complete Jewish Bible version, mean *commandment* and *commandments* (respectively) in Hebrew. The word *torah* is the Hebrew word to describe the first five books of the Bible. In other Bible translations, the word *torah* translates to the word *law*. I prefer using the word *torah*, as it explains in one word that it is the understanding of commandments and guidelines that God gave Moses for the people of Israel to follow and deal with daily life in His righteous way.

When you learn to love our Lord (our Heavenly Father, Jesus (Yeshua) our Brother and Savior, and the Holy Spirit, our internal Comforter and Lover of our soul) with all of your heart and soul (will, mind and emotions); then you will love your neighbor (brother or future husband) as yourself. When you learn how to love God first, then you will learn how to love

Introduction

yourself and subsequently love your neighbor. Your neighbor could be your future husband or a friend or acquaintance who connects you to their friend or acquaintance who could be your future husband. You just never know!

...but with God all things are possible.

Matthew 19:26 (NKJV)

The point is that in order for you, my dear sister, to fill your heart's desire to be purely, genuinely, and intimately loved by a man, you first must learn how to love God. Don't feel picked on, because it's the same order for men, too. When men's hearts and minds are renewed, their change will benefit you, my spiritual sister, as *qualified* bachelors in the Lord will abound. Making Jesus the Lord and Savior of your life is the first and most important decision you can make. The second decision to consider is how to choose someone to be your husband. With the lack of accountability and education, the question you as a *single* person need to ask is, "How do I learn to have appropriate boundaries and make the second most important decision in life?"

It is unfortunate that pastors are not discussing relationships and boundaries from the pulpit for those who are seeking to be married. I am not going to water down the Gospel. Sometimes, we must be real with ourselves as a body of the Messiah (Christ) and confront what could be considered *bad news* head-on so we can know how to live the Good News. The willingness to talk about healthy relationships has become a *dis-ease*. Let me explain.

If the body of Christ is not getting to the root of relationship *dis-ease*, then we as believers in Christ will continue to be just like the world. The way to kill the infection of the *dis-ease* is by getting to the root of the problem by openly discussing this

A Love Letter to the Ladies

topic in the church. We will inevitably be unsuccessful in our romantic relationships and future marriages if we don't.

There are many reasons for unsuccessful relationships, but I believe one of the biggest is that we have more unholy or worldly examples of how to date or court than Godly ones. It is rare to hear advice on dating and courting from our pastors. From the pulpit, some scriptures are taught in a short thity-minute-long to hour-long message, which may or may not be effective. We simply are not hearing enough Godly relationship messages in church. Making it even more difficult for those who are interested in courting someone is the fact that we may not have real-life examples of Christian couples to help guide, counsel, or mentor us. Many churches offer marriage counseling, but instruction on how to live a holy and pure life in Jesus as a single person is rare.

For Christians not to have good examples of people living an undefiled lifestyle doesn't make sense. Secular media and worldly and *fleshly* ways are the options that are bombarding believers on the *how-tos* of dating, courting, and keeping pure before marriage. Oh, my, I don't know about you, my sister, but my own knuckleheaded understanding and emotion-led heart can be the most deceptive of all. Following our own fleshly heart and understanding of love can cause poor decisions that could lead to trouble down the road.

Hollywood and the secular media (television shows, movies, music, magazines, novels, and the internet) with their blatantly sinful portrayal of dating doesn't make the situation any better. Godly dating examples rarely exist; scantily clad men and women, premarital-sex scenes, and pickup lines are common. Seldom can one learn how to date and be blessed with a lifelong partner through the mainstream media.

Then our friends and family give us advice whether we ask

Introduction

for it or not. We rely on their experiences of life and love and apply them to ourselves. Guidance that is good for one person may not be good for someone else. Sometimes, advice based on personal experiences can cause more damage than good. My goodness, it seems to me that advice can be a "lose-lose" situation and a cycle of self-torture and failure that has to end!

As a church, we need to stop denying our continued failures in romantic relationships with the opposite sex. No wonder the divorce rate among believers of Jesus is the same as among *the world*. I think it's obvious we need a revival of revolutionary righteousness in our relationships. If we are learning predominately from the world about romantic relationships, dating, courting, and how to have a successful marriage when the ways of this world system are obviously failing, isn't it foolish to continue learning and following the world's ways?

Now, I am not saying I have the perfect formula or answer for this problem. But, as a born again believer and single man of over twenty-one years the Lord has used me to minister to the body of Christ at the churches I have attended and also outside of the church to both single men and women and even help married couples. But I am saying that together, with the Word of God, the Holy Spirit's guidance, and help from qualified pastors, elders, leaders, and Christian couples that have followed God's plan for relationships and are successful, we too can be victorious.

This book will challenge you, shock you, and maybe even make you laugh and cry. Most importantly, I pray, hope, and believe that it will help you search your heart, mind, and soul to make sure your priorities are in order. Once your priorities are in order and you have placed your full hope and heart in God first, then your heart's desire will come to pass. So, my sister, yield yourself to the Lord, and He will give you the desires and secret petitions of your heart.

> *Commit your way to the Lord [roll and repose each care of your load on Him]; trust [lean on, rely on, and be confident] also in Him and He will bring it to pass.*
>
> Psalm 37:4 (AMP)

The Word of God also states:

> *But seek (aim at and strive after) first His kingdom and His righteousness (His way of doing and being right), and then all these things taken together will be given you besides.*
>
> Matthew 6:32-33 (AMP)

Therefore, my heart's desire is for you to draw closer to our Heavenly Father than ever before. Become the woman of God He has called you to be. Fully trust Him, and give Him the honor to be your Most High Father. Then on your wedding day, He can give you, His highly precious daughter, a man He has deemed worthy of you.

Introduction

A Love Letter to the Ladies

CHAPTER ONE

The Price of Purity

My heartfelt prayer is that every lady recognizes and comes to a full understanding of her true, eternal value as a person. I pray that you will take your position as the daughter of the Most High Father and dance with your Daddy as He gives you your deepest heart's desires. He knows best what you, as a woman, need.

You are Beautiful

Ladies, did you know that your beauty surpasses what the normal man sees? Yes, you may make men turn their heads and say to themselves, "Wow, look what the Lord has done!" But this is a statement about your physical appearance: the makeup on your face, the clothes and jewelry you wear, as well as your body shape and size. But do you understand how special you are in God's eyes?

> *Then your fame went forth among the nations on account of your beauty, for it was perfect because of My splendor which I bestowed on you," declares the Lord GOD.*
>
> Ezekiel 16:14

The Price of Purity

The question is, can you make a man's head turn without showing everything you have physically and make a man seek to find the beauty that supersedes the obvious? That is my challenge to you. Can you go beyond the superficial? Can you make a man desire you without compromising any physical boundaries? In other words, can you make him want to "purchase" the product without giving him a "taste sample," if you will? Oh, my! Did I hit a nerve? Are you angry because the words "purchase" and "taste sample" are used to describe your willingness to compromise your beauty? Well, for those of you who determine the value of a man primarily on the amount of money he makes, the kind of car he owns, and what type of job he has, it would make sense that a man would attempt to put a price on you. Stop reading for the next thirty seconds, and think about that comment for a moment. Think about the value your Most High Father has bestowed upon you, and you will discover how invaluable you truly are, my sister. If you believe in Jesus and have made a commitment to Him, then you are part of the bride of the Messiah. Let me elaborate on this for a moment.

Christ Paid the Price

When you accepted Jesus as your Lord and Savior (born again), you became a new creature in Christ. You were purchased with a price. But the price was not paid with a dollar, yen, pound, or whatever other form of currency the world uses. The price paid for you was the life of our Father's only begotten Son. When Jesus died for you, He died to pay for all your sins and rose again from the dead three days later to show that you are set free from eternal death. Jesus' death is the highest price paid for a wonderful daughter like you. The price of Jesus' death gives you the right to be the bride of the

Messiah. Anyone who believes in the Messiah (Jesus) is His bride. So please understand the value God has placed on you and your life.

The following scripture points out the high price Jesus paid for you:

> *Do you not know that your body is the temple (the very sanctuary) of the Holy Spirit Who lives within you, Whom you have received [as a Gift] from God? You are not your own, You were bought with a price [purchased with a preciousness and paid for, made His own]. So then, honor God and bring glory to Him in your body."*
>
> 1 Corinthians 6:19-20 (AMP)

Your Body is a Holy Temple, so Save it for Marriage

It is important to understand that since Jesus gave His life for you, He asks that you give your all to Him. This includes your body, soul, and spirit unto the Lord Jesus as a living sacrifice. The Amplified Version of the Bible states the following about your body being dedicated for the Father's purposes:

> *Food [is intended] for the stomach and the stomach for food, but God will finally end [the functions of] both and bring them to nothing. The body is not intended for sexual immorality, but [is intended] for the Lord, and the Lord [is intended] for the body [to save, sanctify, and raise it again]. And God both raised the Lord to life and will also raise us up by His power. Do you not see and know that your bodies are members (bodily parts) of Christ (the Messiah)?*
>
> 1 Corinthians 6:13-15

Think about the way you eat. Eating fast food every day would not honor God as you would be abusing your body with poor eating habits. For the ladies who have been blessed with a high metabolism, remember that although you may not see the negative effects of fast food on the exterior of your physical body, your internal organs may certainly be affected. In comparison, it's the same way with sex. If you sleep around with a lot of men, you are increasing your chances of catching a sexually transmitted disease (STD). Even if you have only been with one man, remember the man may have a history with women that you are unaware of and can transfer not only a disease, but a spiritual sickness. Look at 1 Corinthians 6:18:

> *Flee sexual immorality. Every sin that a man does is outside the body, but he who commits sexual immorality sins against his own body.*
>
> (NKJV)

The scripture is a bit of a mystery. Why is sexual immorality the only sin against the body? Why isn't overeating? I truly believe when one has sex with another person, they may be transferring more than just a physical disease. Scientists now know that DNA is transferred as well. Spiritually, unclean spirits may transfer from the person to you. I can tell you from my personal experience that when I was having premarital sex, my personal walk with the Lord was definitely affected. I believe if you are honest with yourself, you would agree that your walk with Jesus was affected as well. Please consider keeping your temple (body) pure for the Holy Spirit.

Our Father has more to say about your body, and He tells us that it should not succumb to your fleshly desires. Romans 6:12–13 in the Amplified Version states:

> *Let not sin therefore rule as king in your mortal (short-lived, perishable) bodies, to make you yield to its cravings and be subject to its lusts and evil passions. Do*

not continue offering or yielding your bodily members [and faculties] to sin as instruments (tools) of wickedness. But offer and yield yourselves to God as though you have been raised from the dead to [perpetual] life, and your bodily members [and faculties] to God, presenting them as implements of righteousness.

And continuing in the Amplified Version Romans 6:19 states:

I am speaking in familiar human terms because of your natural limitations. For as you yielded your bodily members [and faculties] as servants to impurity and ever increasing lawlessness, so now yield your bodily members [and faculties] once for all as servants to righteousness (right being and doing) [which leads] to sanctification.

Honor God by using your body to glorify His name and do His work. Instead of being like the world and even some fellow Christians who don't believe in honoring God with sexual purity, be the standard by following Christ's example. Remember, He wants to reside in a *temple* that is pure and holy as He is Holy. I am not saying you will be perfect and never fall to sin, but I am saying that you do not have to live a promiscuous lifestyle anymore. Ask the Holy Spirit to strengthen you and to use you for His purposes.

Love is Patient

Now, I know that is intense. I believe God has made it clear through the scripture that your body is not only yours but more importantly, His. Guess what? For those of you who have a desire to have a family and experience the wonderful blessing of what I refer to as sanctified sex or clean consummation, your body is not yours to give away before marriage, even to the man who gave you a promise or engagement ring as a statement that he is going to marry you. If you truly love each other and more importantly, if you both truly love your Father's ultimate sacrifice of His Son and your Savior Jesus, you will be a living example of what 1 Corinthians 13:4-5 states:

> *Love is patient, love is kind and is not jealous; love does not brag and is not arrogant, does not act unbecomingly; it does not seek its own, is not provoked, does not take into account a wrong suffered ...*

Look specifically at the first verse; it states love is patient. Do you believe you are being patient when you say, "Well, how do I know if I am going to like it (sex) without taking a test drive?" Don't misunderstand me; it is normal for two people who truly care for one another to have the desire to express themselves in a physically intimate interaction, but that expression is to be saved for the day the full commitment is made, the day of marriage. Now this is where it gets tricky. If you were wondering if the man is someone you would marry, let me pose a question. This is straight up. If you are not sure you would marry the man, then why would you be open to having a physical relationship with the same person? You are worth much more than a moment of sexual passion. Let me remind you, my dear sister . . . if the man claims he loves you but is not willing to wait, or he is willing to put you in a compromising situation, then you need to wonder if he really loves you. For example, if the man keeps inviting you over to his house to be alone with him and makes advances toward you, then you may truly want to consider this question: "When he says to me that he loves me and is willing to wait, why does he keep pushing my physical boundaries further and further each time?" Proverbs 26:24 states:

A Love Letter to the Ladies

*A malicious man disguises himself with his lips, but in his **heart** he harbors deceit.*

(NIV)

Love is patient as it states in 1 Corinthians 13:4. Verse five states that love does not act unbecomingly; it does not seek its own, is not provoked ...

1 John 2:3-6 states:

We know that we have come to know him if we obey his commands. The man who says, "I know him," but does not do what he commands is a liar, and the truth is not in him. But if anyone obeys his word, God's love is truly made complete in him. This is how we know we are in him: Whoever claims to live in him must walk as Jesus did.

(NIV)

Those verses don't leave much room for any justification. If the man is not obeying the scriptures, which is to say waiting to have sex until marriage, then he is a liar, and the truth is not in him. He is a liar. Take a look at what Paul says under the direction of the Holy Spirit in 1 Corinthians 7:7-9:

Sometimes I wish everyone were single like me – a simpler life in many ways! But celibacy is not for everyone any more than marriage is. God gives the gift of the single life to some, the gift of the married life to others.

It continues in verse ten.

I do, though, tell the unmarried and widows that singleness might well be the best thing for them, as it has been for me. But if they can't manage their desires and emotions, they should by all means go ahead and get married. *The difficulties of marriage are preferable by far to a sexually tortured life as a single.*

(The Message)

For those of you who want to know the answer to the question, "What is okay or an appropriate way to physically express my love for my boyfriend or fiancé without it being wrong in my Heavenly Father's eyes?" I say be patient, as boundaries will be discussed in a future chapter. Now, my dear sister, if the man cannot respect the Word of God, then toss him out. Drop him. Seriously. Love does not act unbecomingly. What is unbecomingly? According to Merriam-Webster Dictionary, the word unbecoming means "behavior or language that does not suit one's character." If the man you are courting is claiming to be a true follower of Jesus, then his behavior and language should fit the character of a Christian. Look back at 1 Corinthians 13:5. Right after the word unbecomingly, the following six words are the key to whether a man truly loves you: "It [love] does not seek its own." Wow! In other words, love is not selfish. Galatians 5:24 in the Amplified Bible states:

And those who belong to Christ Jesus (the Messiah) have crucified the flesh (the godless human nature) with its passions and appetites and desires.

Let's get real here. God made you to have normal passions, appetites, and desires. There is nothing wrong with having these normal human wants. The question is: "Are you willing to withhold those normal wants and bear your own cross and crucify your flesh?" Romans 12:1 beautifully states:

I appeal to you therefore, brethren, and beg of you in view of [all] the mercies of God, to make a decisive dedication of your bodies [presenting all your members and faculties] as a living sacrifice, holy (devoted, consecrated) and well pleasing to God, which is your reasonable (rational, intelligent) service and spiritual worship.

(AMP)

Remember, God is realistic, and He made you to have certain desires. Please hear my heart for you, Sister: He wants to bless you so that you can express these desires freely and enjoy them in the sanctity of marriage. Stay strong. Don't let the man who says he loves you persuade you with words like, "Well, we will eventually get married, and God understands." No! No! No! Those are words from an impatient man. Once you give yourself to him, there will be little or nothing else special about you to keep for the wedding night. Seriously.

Most men think (especially men who are not fully committed to Jesus) that if they already have all the *benefits* of a woman without being legally committed to her in a marriage, then why rush to the marriage altar? It's sad but true. Consider this. The man has your heart, time, admiration, attention, and spirit; and for some of you, maybe you are cooking, ironing, and cleaning. Now he has your body, too. I know this is tough to hear, but the man has pretty much acquired everything from you physically and emotionally without a marriage proposal.

Or, for those who are engaged, he has it all without a wedding date. For those of you who already have a date set for your wedding and may be thinking, "He has committed to me and we are getting married soon, so a little 'sugar from the wedding cake' before the wedding ceremony is alright!" Nope, not if you aren't married yet. If the pastor or priest hasn't said, "You may now kiss the bride," then you need to tell your future husband and yourself to keep your hands, mouth, and other body parts to yourselves. Yes, the flesh (physical body) and your five senses want it now. God understands. Look at Proverbs 13:12:

Hope deferred makes the heart sick, but desire fulfilled is a tree of life.

As you are obedient to God's instructions, your desire will be fulfilled as the scripture states. Like a tree of life. And yes, with some nice, tasty fruit, too. Don't worry. I've got good news for you. Your hands, mouth, and other body parts will all work on your honeymoon night, maybe not in perfect harmony, but they will work. God made it that way. Just imagine how awesome the experience will be because you both waited with purity, respect, honor, anticipation, and love for one another. Think of the great joy you will have learning how to explore and pleasure one another. Hold on to Galatians 6:9. It states:

> *And let us not lose heart and grow weary and faint in acting nobly and doing right, for in due time and at the appointed season we shall reap, if we do not loosen and relax our courage and faint.*
>
> (AMP)

Love is patient. Wait for your husband and keep yourself pure for him. Believe me … God is going to honor you with your heart's desires. I'm sure you've heard the saying "The best things come to those who wait." That is definitely true. Start thanking and praising your Father ahead of time for the one you have been longing for all your life. He's coming. Just be patient. He is worth it. Don't forget that you are the daughter of the Most High Father. You are very valuable and worth the wait. Make the man work hard and prove his love to you. If he truly is a man after God's heart, he won't play with your heart and lead you to compromise your purity and integrity. Brienne Murk, in her book *Eyes Wide Open* wonderfully explains,

> *"Like so many others, I used to think that purity was about sex. I thought that if I stayed a virgin until I got married, I'd be pure. In the last few years, however, I've realized that true purity is not connected merely to our sexuality, but to every part of our lives. Purity has to do with movies we watch, books we read, clothes we wear, friends we hang out with, words we say, places we go,*

people we date, and things we do. Purity has to do with how we think, what we nurture inside our hearts, and how we express our passions and desires. Purity has to do with refusing to give our hearts to people who aren't worthy to be entrusted with such a precious gift, and instead waiting for the man or woman who will spend his or her entire life cherishing us with godly, tender affection."

There is a price to pay for purity. Paul tells us to count the cost. Not only is this statement for following Christ, but it can be applied to abstaining from premarital sex. Wow, think of it! God will honor both of you with the greatest emotional and physical intimacy because of your patience and willingness to wait for one another. Praise the Creator of true intimacy!

The Price of Purity

A Love Letter to the Ladies

Chapter One: Reflections

Take time to reflect on the following questions and scripture reference.

- What are the three main reasons why we as Christian singles should remain sexually pure?
- What are three main beneficial blessings of remaining sexually pure?

Scripture to meditate on:

*My old self has been crucified with Christ. It is no longer I who live, but Christ lives in me. So I live in this earthly **body** by trusting in the Son of God, who loved me and gave himself for me.*

Galatians 2:20 (NLT)

The Price of Purity

CHAPTER TWO

Turn Your Pain into Power

God is a God of forgiveness. Many people have a hard time accepting the forgiveness of God, which is made available through the sacrificial death and resurrection of the perfect and Holy One, Jesus. These people, including me, think we deserve judgment and should spend our life without God in hell due to the severe pain we have caused others. Fortunately, there is great news for those who struggle with this thought. Let's read an incredible biblical story found in Luke 7:36-50:

> *Now one of the Pharisees was requesting Him (Jesus) to dine with him, and He entered the Pharisee's house and reclined at the table. And there was a woman in the city who was a sinner; and when she learned that He was reclining at the table in the Pharisee's house, she brought an alabaster vial of perfume, and standing behind Him at His feet, weeping, she began to wet His feet with her tears, and kept wiping them with the hair of her head, and kissing His feet and anointing them with the perfume. Now when the Pharisee who had invited Him saw this,*

he said to himself, "If this man were a prophet, He would know who and what sort of person this woman is who is touching Him, that she is a sinner."

And Jesus answered him, "Simon, I have something to say to you." And he replied, "Say it, Teacher."

"A moneylender had two debtors: one owed five hundred denarii, and the other fifty. When they were unable to repay, he graciously forgave them both. So which of them will love him more?"

Simon answered and said, "I suppose the one whom he forgave more."

And He said to him, "You have judged correctly." Turning toward the woman, He said to Simon, "Do you see this woman? I entered your house; you gave Me no water for My feet, but she has wet My feet with her tears and wiped them with her hair. You gave Me no kiss; but she, since the time I came in, has not ceased to kiss My feet. You did not anoint My head with oil, but she anointed My feet with perfume. For this reason I say to you, her sins, which are many, have been forgiven, for she loved much; but he who is forgiven little, loves little." Then He said to her, "Your sins have been forgiven." Those who were reclining at the table with Him began to say to themselves, "Who is this man who even forgives sins?" And He said to the woman, "Your faith has saved you; go in peace."

    No matter what type of sin or how many sins one has committed, God has already forgiven you. Some people think that forgiveness is heresy; but please hear me out. From a spiritual point of view, when Jesus died on the cross, all sins were paid for when He said, "It is finished." This means when

A Love Letter to the Ladies

He died on the cross, He took our place for every single sin we committed in the past, sins we commit in the present, and any that will be committed in the future. It includes every sin committed against us, past, present, and future, as well. So, spiritually speaking, for those who have been offended, victimized, used, assaulted, lied to, gossiped about, betrayed, raped, killed, etc., God the Son paid the price for everyone by dying on the cross. That price was for both you and the crime's perpetrator.

For those of you who have been hurt by others, this may be hard to believe, but forgiveness doesn't mean that He looks lightly at how you have been wronged. Let's look at sin through our Heavenly Father's eyes, from His perspective. You send Your only Son, who has been with You since before creation, has never wronged anyone, is sinless and living as One with You in the Spirit. Then You (God) send Your only Son (Jesus) to the earth, only to be offended, victimized, used, assaulted, lied to, gossiped about, betrayed, killed, etc. Isaiah 53:10, if read out of context can be disturbing or misunderstood. The scripture reads,

But the LORD was pleased to crush Him, putting Him to grief;

If you only read the first part of the sentence, you may think to yourself, "What kind of demented Father would say that He was pleased to inflict pain and allow His Son to sacrifice Himself?" But as you finish reading the verse in Isaiah 53:10 and continue with verses eleven through twelve, then the word is in context.

If He would render Himself as a guilt offering, He will see His offspring, He will prolong His days, And the good pleasure of the LORD will prosper in His hand. As a result of the anguish of His soul, He will see it

and be satisfied; By His knowledge the Righteous One, My Servant, will justify the many, As He will bear their iniquities. Therefore, I will allot Him a portion with the great, And He will divide the booty with the strong; Because He poured out Himself to death, And was numbered with the transgressors; Yet He Himself bore the sin of many, And interceded for the transgressors.

The key to the scripture is Our Heavenly Father and His Son, our Savior and Bridegroom, Jesus knew that He must lay His life down for us, His own bride. That's incredible love! In other words, Jesus died once for everyone's sins; those committed against us and those we commit toward others.

So, my sister, the reason the woman broke a year's salary worth of her perfume was to anoint the head of her Bridegroom and wash His feet with her tears and hair. The disciples took offense, saying that this costly perfume could have been sold and the money given to the poor (Mark 26:13). Although they had good intentions, they missed the point. Jesus and this sinner both knew what her act meant. This was her personal sacrifice and expression to her Lord and Savior who was about to take her place in death and pay the price for all her sins. It was not a wasteful act. She understood the price unto death that was going to be paid for her, and it was the least she could do to honor the Lover of her soul by using her hard-earned perfume to prepare His body for burial.

Only she and Jesus knew how much He set her free. Only you and Jesus know how much He has set you free from the bondage you were experiencing. His death sets each us of us free. His death was not in vain but done in love, His greatest gift to us. This type of love is known as *agape*, or unconditional love. It is the love that each of us at some point (whether we know it or not) have been looking for and it is available only through Jesus.

A Love Letter to the Ladies

Had I been given the opportunity to speak to the *sinner* lady who gave this offering unto Jesus, I would say this, "I wrap my arms around my sister who broke her alabaster box and used her hair to anoint Jesus' feet! I say to you that I completely understand why you would do such a thing. Only you know, Sister, every single sin that He has forgiven you of, and not only that, but delivered you, set you free and also gave you power over that sin to go and sin no more."

God doesn't want you to forget your deliverance. Carry your cross and place those painful experiences of the past on your back. Forgiveness is about you no longer being enslaved to the emotions of bitterness, hatefulness, and resentment against the one who has sinned against you. What do I mean when I say enslaved? The person who sinned against you seven years ago has more than likely moved on with living their life. Unfortunately, you may have been holding on to your memories and allowing them to preoccupy your mind at times, and it has affected not only your current relationships but also even your physical health. The good news is by forgiving the one who has sinned against you, you have become empowered. You have now taken back control by moving on with your life and not letting that past hurt control your emotions. You are overcoming the temptation of being bitter, and this will allow you to teach others how to do the same.

Be ready to administer the balm of Gilead of your personal healing experience to those who are trapped with those same sins. Grab their hand and pull them out of their pit. Remember, God the Father's pleasure is to see His Son fulfill the ultimate will of sacrifice for our sins; not because He was a sadist (one who gets pleasure from causing or seeing someone go through pain), but because He saw past the pain that Jesus was suffering. Look closely. If God would have stopped time (pressed pause on the DVD if you will) and said, "Nope, the pain My Son is going through is too much, and I'm going to strike down all of His accusers and let Him go free," that would have been the most selfish decision He could have made. He saw that His Son was beaten down with our sins; yet we are the same ones who call out to Jesus to be set free.

Don't be selfish; help your sister get out of her sins. Whether it be drugs, pride of life (look how beautiful I am), premarital sex, holding hatred for the person who sexually assaulted her, self-hatred and blaming herself for being sexually assaulted, greed, or any addiction, help her in any way you can. Don't let your past sin and her current sin keep you from helping her. Don't be afraid to remember the sin from which Jesus set you free. Be willing to bare the pain of your memories; but this time the memories will be used to help someone else. When you trust your Father in heaven about the memory, it will strengthen you and encourage the other person. He has given you His Spirit. Remember His words to you which are found in 2 Timothy 1:3-7:

> *I thank God, whom I serve with a pure conscience, as my forefathers did, as without ceasing I remember you in my prayers night and day, greatly desiring to see you, being mindful of your tears, that I may be filled with joy when I call to remembrance the genuine faith that is in you, which dwelt first in your grandmother Lois and your mother Eunice, and I am persuaded is in you also. Therefore I remind you to stir up the gift of God which is in you through the laying on of my hands. For God has not given us a spirit of fear, but of power and of love and of a sound mind.*
>
> (NKJV)

There are some key words and steps that Paul discusses about interceding with our Savior in order to win and deliver souls. Let's follow the verses one by one in order to understand what Paul is saying and the revelation God gave me regarding the scriptures. Verse three states:

... remember you in my prayers night and day ...

Paul states he was dedicating much time through praying. Using Paul's example, pray first for the girl or woman whom God has placed in your path who is experiencing the same thing you suffered. It might not be easy, but His yoke is easy, and His burden is light. In verse four, he mentions:

... greatly desiring to see you ...

Have a genuine desire to see the person come out of their bondage.

Verse four continues:

... being mindful of your tears ...

Also, be mindful of *her* tears ... remember the pain you experienced so you will have compassion on her and her pain. The verse finishes with:

... that I may be filled with joy ...

What!? Filled with joy by remembering the pain that the woman is going through? That doesn't make sense. My revelation of this portion of the scripture is this: Paul is saying he receives joy in sharing with the suffering of those who are in pain, because it leads to healing. If the woman you are ministering to was affected by someone else's actions (i.e. sexual assault, domestic violence, abandonment, etc.) and you experienced the same suffering and were set free, when you experience it with her, it will be healing for both of you. An understanding of joy and love caused by pain will start to unfold. God never said that His love would be painless. Use the past pain to produce pleasure and prosperity in the soul to the one you are ministering. His love is marvelous.

Now, I understand that I may make this sound easier said than done. I am not denying the fact that you may still have a hard time dealing with your anger for the hurt that has been done to you. You have the right to be angry. Okay, I might've hit a nerve, and you may be thinking to yourself, *Who are you to tell me that I have to go through the pain of remembering that worthless, scum of the earth, who perpetrated this crime against me?* That is understandable. The truth is, I understand why you would be very angry. In fact, your Father in heaven is raging with fire at that person. Remember Yeshua, Jesus, when He said:

> *But whoso shall offend one of these little ones which believe in me, it were better for him that a millstone were hanged about his neck, and that he were drowned in the depth of the sea.*
>
> Matthew 18:6 (KJV)

Let me give you one of the most extreme examples of what most of society sees as an unforgiveable sin: child molestation. In fact, it incites the rage of your Heavenly Father, the Father of all children who are being violated night and day by the enemy, Satan himself, through men and women who willfully choose to assault them. How someone can justify such a disgusting act, only the perpetrator knows. The question one may ask themselves is, *Why doesn't the Father in heaven do anything to prevent it? Why can't He just cause that person to die of a heart attack or be struck by a car, or do whatever it takes before the person gets close to hurting a child?* Those are questions many people ask. With questions, we try to understand why God allows terrible things to happen.

A Love Letter to the Ladies

The truth is, when I was no older than four years old, I witnessed what no young boy or girl should see. At seven years old, something else happened to me that a child should never have to experience. In the next chapter, I will share a very personal account from my life so you are able to read firsthand the pain I went through in the past and how God healed me.

My story will ideally help you understand how the devil works in someone's life at a very young age. It will explain how the enemy will do anything to pervert the truth and keep someone from knowing how to love with a pure heart. I was a little boy simply trying to figure out how to love a girl. Warning: it is very graphic and emotional. Take a moment to pray before you continue reading. Here we go. Welcome to my memories, from which I've been healed. Know there is hope.

Turn Your Pain into Power

A Love Letter to the Ladies

Chapter Two: Reflections

Take time to reflect on the following questions and scripture reference.

- What are some of the reasons I should forgive all those who have offended me, especially the ones who have violated me when I have done absolutely nothing wrong to them?
- When I forgive someone, does that mean I have to continue to spend time with the person or put myself in a position where I may be hurt again?

Scripture to meditate on:

Forgive us what we have done wrong, as we too have forgiven those who have wronged us.
Matthew 6:12 (CJB)

CHAPTER THREE

My Personal Story of Pain

The earliest memory that shaped my thought processes about love and sex began when I was about two years old; my mommy was pregnant with my sister. For no reason that I was aware, I remember my daddy became angry with my mommy. He grabbed the rocking chair and threw it at us, as I was in her arms. Even now, I have flashbacks of the chair flying toward us.

At the age of three, I experienced another incident that helped shape my early understanding of love. My daddy arrived home from work. He had been drinking. He started yelling at my mommy, pushing her for no reason. I knew what these actions meant, as I had seen them before. I had instructions from my mommy: if daddy became violent, I was to grab my baby sister, go to my bedroom, shut the door, and play with the toys in my big football-shaped toy box. I followed the instructions and grabbed my six-month-old sister, put her on my blanket, and dragged the blanket into my room like a heavy sack of potatoes.

My Personal Story of Pain

   This particular time, my daddy beat up my mommy badly, and I remember flinching every time I heard a smack or a thud. I knew he was throwing my mommy against the wall. I didn't understand why my daddy would do this to her. I was confused. After beating my mommy, my daddy came into my room and told me to go to the kitchen and eat. As I walked into the kitchen, I saw my mommy's bloody and bruised face. He sat me in a chair at the kitchen table across from him. My mommy was making him a sandwich to eat. My daddy's back was toward her in the kitchen, but I was facing her, and I saw her pain as she shook while spreading mayonnaise on the bread for his sandwich.

   My daddy spoke to me and said, "See, Mijo (*my son*, in Spanish), this is the way you love a woman."

   I listened to him, but I wondered why he was saying such a thing. I felt confused because he was telling me the way I love a woman is by beating a girl up like he does my mommy. My mommy continued making the sandwich by cutting tomatoes for it. Suddenly, she stopped slicing the tomatoes, turned around with the knife in her hand, and started to walk slowly toward my daddy as he continued talking to me. As she walked closer to where my daddy sat, her face was full of anger. The closer she got to my daddy, the more nervous and excited I became.

   This was the man who continually locked us up in our own home like prisoners. The house had bars on the windows without any latch to escape in case of emergency and a padlock that locked from the outside only. These were to keep us inside while my daddy was at work. He is the man who beat my mommy almost daily and threw chairs, tables, and other objects to hurt us.

   With the knife raised over her head, she continued to sneak

up on him. My eyes were wide, and I started to nod my head yes in approval. Right then, my mommy plunged the knife down toward my daddy to stab him in the back. But he saw me shaking my head and moved, getting stabbed in the shoulder instead of the back or neck like my mother had intended.

I remember my daddy moaning in pain as I sat there in shock. My mommy was yelling at him, saying, "Don't you ever tell my son anything like that again. You're lucky I didn't kill you, you bastard!"

My father called 911, and the police arrived at the house within minutes. They started asking my mommy questions. "Did you stab him?"

"Hell yeah, I stabbed him! What do you expect me to do?" she replied.

They walked over to her, placed her wrists in handcuffs, and said, "You are being arrested for attempted murder."

My dad just stood there quietly. I ran over to my mom and grabbed her leg as I dragged my sister on my blanket right next to me.

"Okay, Mommy, I am ready to go with you," I exclaimed.

"Um, I am sorry, little guy, but you cannot go with her," the officer said.

"No. I am not going to let her go. I go with her!" I cried. "Take my daddy, not my mommy!" I pleaded.

I started to cry as the police tried to detach my arms from around her leg. I refused to let go. Before the police could separate my mother and me, a darker-skinned officer walked into the house and noticed what was happening. He saw my

My Personal Story of Pain

mommy's busted face, closed black eye, and bruises all over her body. Suddenly a voice spoke. "Take me in, it is my fault. She was defending herself," my daddy admitted.

Handcuffs were placed immediately on my daddy's wrists, and he was taken away in a cop car. About a week later, my daddy got out of jail and returned home. The cycle of physical and verbal abuse began again between my parents; but about six months later, my mommy got a divorce. Finally!

A few months after the divorce, I was in my room with my one-year-old sister. She was lying on the bed, and I started to jump on her like she was a trampoline.

Suddenly I heard my mommy say, "Mijo! What are you doing? Stop it! Why did you do that to your sister?"

I said, "Because Daddy said that's the way I show her love."

She said, "No, Mijo. That's not the way you love your sister."

That was the first and last time I did any harmful act to my sister (or any other woman); but even after my mommy's comments, I was never shown or told how to truly love my sister.

My people are ruined because they don't know what's right or true.

Hosea 4:6 (The Message)

At an early age, the enemy, also known as Satan, tried planting a seed of violence in me. I thank Jesus that my mother saw what I was innocently doing and corrected me. The dilemma I faced at a young age was that I still didn't know how to express my love toward my sister, or any girl, for that matter. My next experience of learning about loving a woman came from my grandpa. This story is also graphic. I'm sharing this to help you to understand what Satan tried to do in me and how God's grace and mercy made me an overcomer, so that you can be an overcomer, too. As a woman, you need to know how a man should treat you.

Aha! This Must Be Love

I lived at my grandparents' house with my mom and sister when I was seven years old. One day, I was looking for my grandpa. I entered my cousin Adrina's bedroom and found him watching TV.

"Hey, Grandpa! What are you watching?" I ask.

"T.J., you need to leave. Go play," he replied.

"Ah, Grandpa. Why? I want to stay and watch TV with you."

He responded to my comment with, "You should go."

"Come on, Grandpa," I pled.

He resigned and said, "Okay, shut the door."

I think, *Cool! I love doing things and spending time with my grandpa. He makes me feel important, accepted, and loved. He is the only male figure in my life since my mom divorced my dad.* I sat on the bed next to my grandpa, and we watched TV.

Wow! *What are that boy and girl doing lying in bed together?* I asked myself. They didn't have any clothes on. I was confused, excited, and curious. They were kissing and touching one another all over their bodies. I wondered what they were doing. It looked really neat and fun. My grandpa was watching the show and drinking his beer. He really seemed to like what he was watching, as he had not said a word and he kept his eyes on the TV.

The door opened.

My Personal Story of Pain

"Hey, T.J. and Grandpa! What are you doing?" my cousin asked.

"Adrina, get out of here!" Grandpa said. I was surprised, confused, and angry.

"No, Grandpa, why can't she stay in here with us and watch TV?"

"No, both of you get out of here now! You have to leave! Go, get out of here now!" he said as his irritation grew.

"Ah, man, come on, Grandpa," I replied.

"Go," he said as he shut the door. I was confused, angry, hurt, and rejected. Five minutes later …

"Hey, Grandpa, it's just me. I want to watch TV with you. Adrina isn't with me," I told him through the door.

"Come in and shut the door, Mijo," he said.

I felt accepted, excited, and loved again. I looked at the TV as I walked toward him and noticed that he was still watching the same channel. I noticed it was channel twenty-seven, and I read on the screen, "The Playboy Channel." *Cool, this is the way a boy plays with a girl*, I reconciled. I felt smart, excited, and very curious. I sat next to him again. The boy and girl were wrestling naked. He was on top of her, and they were playing and having fun. They were making sounds, and it looked like fun.

"T.J., there you are!" Adrina said.

"Adrina, no, you can't be in here. Get out," Grandpa said excitedly.

"T.J., move the hide-a-bed in front of the door," he instructed.

A Love Letter to the Ladies

"Sorry, Mija, you have to stay out."

"Grandpa ..." Adrina said as she was trying to push the door open. I was leaning against the hide-a-bed as it was pushed against the door.

"Nope, you can't watch this with us. It's only for boys," he stated.

"That's not fair. I'm telling Grandma," she said in frustration as she walked away from the blocked door.

I sat back on the bed with my grandpa and continued to watch the boy and girl wrestle again. It was neat and looked like fun. They seemed to love each other. I felt loved, accepted, special, excited, curious, and relieved at that moment. I felt special because I got to hang out with Grandpa all by myself.

Suddenly we heard, "Bob, why is this bed against the door? Move it right now!" my grandma said.

My grandpa turned off the TV and got up quickly to move the bed from blocking the door. I was anxious, scared, excited, and confused, because grandpa was acting nervous, as if we were doing something he wasn't supposed to be doing.

My grandma was standing in the doorway with Adrina behind her.

"What were you watching? You were watching that crap again, weren't you?" my grandma said as she grabbed the remote. She turned the TV on to check the channel and then turned it off quickly.

"I can't believe you were watching this with T.J. in the room with you! That's it, I am calling the cable company, and we are getting this channel removed!" she said.

"You guys go play now," Grandma instructed my cousin and me.

33

My Personal Story of Pain

I was angry. Angry because Adrina told Grandma. She did that because she was jealous that I was spending time with Grandpa alone.

"Come on, Adrina, let's go play house," I said to her.

At seven years old, I learned and understood that the way to express my love to my cousin was by playing house. But playing house to me was not your normal *Brady Bunch* type of family interaction. It was more imitating what I saw on the Playboy channel.

Watching pornography that afternoon took my sexual purity from me. Imagine seeing for the very first time a woman and a man naked when you are only seven years old. I saw them doing things I had never seen before. A heightened sense of excitement was within me, and I didn't understand why. I wanted to do the same thing with my cousin to show her how much I loved her, but obviously that wasn't love. Unfortunately, the cycle of lost innocence continued.

The first time I encountered my grandpa watching the Playboy Channel, he told me to leave. I bothered him to a point that he allowed me to watch the channel with him. My grandpa as an adult should have protected me from seeing things like that on television. Regrettably, he allowed my eyes to be sexually assaulted by exposing me to the demons of lust, perversion, voyeurism, and confusion. Satan took my innocence for a second time.

When my father and my mother forsake me, then the LORD will take me up.
Psalm 27:10 (KJV)

Between the two recounted experiences, I witnessed extremes of physicality between a man and a woman: extreme violence and extreme sexual expression. This was total confusion for a young mind that was still developing. But God is faithful, and He will make right the wrongs in our life. He did with me. Romans 8:28 states:

And we know that God causes all things to work together for good to those who love God, to those who are called according to His purpose.

In order to make the unfortunate events work together for the good in my life, God gave me a choice. I could forgive my father and grandfather for exposing me to graphic violence and sexuality at such a young age, or I could hold on to bitterness and resentment in my heart toward them both. When I was young in the Lord, only about six months after I started my personal relationship with God through Jesus Christ, the Holy Spirit told me that I need to forgive my father.

At first my reaction was, "Lord, how dare you tell me I need to forgive my father? You know how much pain he has caused me and my mom."

Then the Lord said, "Yes, I do know. I also know how much I have forgiven you for all of the pain you have caused to others."

Then I thought, *Well, you are right, Lord.*

"If you forgive those who sin against you, your heavenly Father will forgive you. But if you refuse to forgive others, your Father will not forgive your sins."

Matthew 6:14–15 (NLT)

So I reached out to my father, called him and said, "I called you to let you know God told me I need to forgive you for all of the sin and wrongs you did to me and my mom, and so I am. I also ask if you would forgive me for holding hatred, bitterness, and resentment in my heart toward you."

My Personal Story of Pain

He said, "Okay, Mijo. Thank you, and I understand."

Then about a year later, my sister began to tell me about her relationship with him, and she told me how cool he was. I began to get curious, a bit jealous, and to feel like I wanted a relationship with him, too. On my twenty-first birthday, the phone rang, and I noticed on the caller ID it was my father. I picked up the phone, and he said, "Happy birthday, Son!"

He was the first one to call me that morning to wish me a happy birthday, and that meant so much to me. Then he asked, "So what are you going to do for your birthday today?"

I said, "Nothing, really. I'm just going to mow my grandma's lawn."

Then he said, "Would you like some help?"

I said, "Sure."

So he came over and helped me. Then he asked, "Now that we are done, are you hungry? Would you like to go out for lunch?"

I said, "Yeah, that would be great."

So we went out to lunch. While talking and eating, I asked, "Have you ever given your life to Jesus and asked Him to be your personal Lord, God, and Savior?"

He looked at me as his eyes started to water and said, "Look at my arms."

I could see the goosebumps on them. He said, "My coworker was talking to me about having a personal relationship with God and receiving Jesus as my Savior. He offered to pray with me. So I prayed with him, and, yes, I believe in Him."

I asked, "How long ago was this?"

He said, "About a year ago." I said, "Wow! That is around the same time when I called you and asked you to forgive me and also told you that I forgive you for all the past hurts you caused me and Mom."

He said, "Yes, Mijo. That is right!"

See how the power of God and forgiveness goes beyond all human comprehension. Now I love my father and am grateful that I have a relationship with him.

Also, I chose to forgive my grandfather after he passed away, for taking away my innocence. For my own closure, I wrote a letter to him even though he had died. By writing the letter, I no longer allowed myself to be in bondage from the painful memories he had caused me.

You have the same choice. You may be at a fork in the road. One sign says *the never-ending bitter road*, and the other says *forgiveness and compassion for yourself and others*. Please, my sister, choose the path of freedom and empowerment. Choose the golden path of forgiveness and compassion. Remember what Jesus said in Luke 23:34:

Father, forgive them: for they do not know what they are doing.

Have the same heart as Jesus so you can move forward toward your healing. Release the bitterness and resentment, and begin your walk of freedom today. Take the power back from the devil, the power and authority that belong to you in Jesus' name. Increase your freedom by helping other sisters who have been hurt the same way you have been. Show them how you have reached true freedom and empowerment by your choice of forgiveness. When you forgive, it gives you the ability to know true, intimate love. Your heart is softened and no longer hardened by bitterness and resentfulness. When you can receive love, your heart not only allows you to love in your relationship with your earthly father but also your Heavenly Father. Not to mention, you are able to love in your romantic relationships as well. To be a vessel to pour out and receive true, intimate love, being set free from the power of painful negative emotions is imperative.

Chapter Three: Reflections

Take time to reflect on the following questions and scripture references.

- How am I supposed to make sense of my own past personal story of pain and why God allowed those things to happen to me?
- Why is it important for me to forgive the person who has hurt me so badly?

Scripture to meditate on:

Even if that person wrongs you seven times a day and each time turns again and asks forgiveness, you must forgive.
Luke 17:4 (NLT)

Be kind and compassionate to one another, forgiving each other, just as in Christ God forgave you.
Ephesians 4:32 (NIV)

My Personal Story of Pain

CHAPTER FOUR

Eternal Intimacy Brings True Harmony

Well, my sisters, now I write to you about intimacy. There are different ways people view intimacy. Unfortunately, due to the world's influence, we (people who are striving for a pure intimacy) have a difficult time finding it. I ask people what intimacy means to them personally, and most will describe it as involving some sort of physical connection with someone, which usually includes sex. My sisters, I believe you know intimacy is more than sex. Intimacy is something much deeper.

Merriam-Webster Dictionary states the definition of intimacy as, "something of a personal or private nature." Now, let's look further at the root word of *intimacy*, which is *intimate*. It gives two fascinating definitions for the verb *intimate*. Check it out:

1: to make known especially publicly or formally

2: to communicate delicately and indirectly

Be patient with me here. Let's look at the definition of *intimate* as an adjective:

Eternal Intimacy Brings True Harmony

1a: intrinsic, essential

b: belonging to or characterizing one's deepest nature

2: marked by very close association, contact, or familiarity

3a: marked by a warm friendship developing through long association

b: suggesting informal warmth or privacy

4: of a very personal or private nature

Okay, now here is the definition of *intimate* as a noun:

a very close friend or confidant

Not one of these definitions mentions anything about physical touch or sexual expression. Very interesting! Of course, intimacy may be expressed with physical touch, both nonsexual and sexual expression. These expressions of intimacy depend on the type of interpersonal relationships you encounter. An example of familiar intimacy is encouraging a friend who is going through some difficult times: you may place your hand on their shoulder as you speak. That is a form of being intimate, but as a friend.

In contrast, a relationship with your husband is intimate in a personal, private way. Now, I said your **husband**, not your boyfriend with a promise ring, not your fiancé with an engagement ring—you know where I am going with the husband comment; I won't go there again. You and your husband have the blessed right to express your deepest emotions to one another without any physical boundaries. That is of course as long as neither of you pushes the limit and makes the other feel uncomfortable. There are still appropriate boundaries within a marriage relationship, but that subject is for another book. Check out Hebrews 13:4. It states:

Marriage is to be held in honor among all, and the marriage bed is to be undefiled; for fornicators and adulterers God will judge.

Therefore what you and your husband do in your marriage bed is blessed; enough said. Now back to intimacy. As mentioned earlier, the type of intimacy you experience will depend on the relationship you have with the other person. Whatever the relationship, intimacy is complicated because it involves the heart.

Oh, boy, look out now! I'm going to be brutally honest going forward. There is no turning back if you want to be real and healed of past relational hurts. May our Comforter, the Holy Spirit, continue to use me as I write. Are you ready for some truth? Okay, here we go …

I love the word intimacy. Listen to the way it sounds: "in-ti-ma-see." Now it sounds close to "in-to-me-see" or "into me see." It's like saying to someone we trust, "Into me see." We need to trust Jesus, our first Love, the One who first loved us; it tells Him that we love Him. When we give Him permission to look into the deepest part of our heart, and we say, "Look into me and see," our trust blesses Him. We need to allow Jesus to go into the dark parts of our hearts; the areas that we prematurely gave to the enemy. The scripture that reminds us of how lost we can become when we fall into the temptation of sin is found in Isaiah 47:10:

You felt secure in your wickedness and said, "No one sees me." Your wisdom and your knowledge, they have deluded you; For you have said in your heart, "I am, and there is no one besides me."

The scripture exposes how our heart gets secure in our own self-deception. It states that we believe no one sees, but God's

Eternal Intimacy Brings True Harmony

intimacy (into me see), states otherwise. We think God doesn't see us when we are sinning. You know and recognize the actions that brought you into the sinful cycle. You want to stop yourself before you fall into the same trap again. You want to break the cycle. It's going to be a battle. Keep in mind this is not only a battle of the flesh, but of the Spirit.

The battle won't be easy; in fact, it can become messy and dirty at times, but remember you are an overcomer. If you are unfamiliar with the armor of God, read Ephesians 6:13-18. Pray the scripture. Once you have prayed the armor of God on you, it is always on you. This is an act of faith, in and of itself. But if you want to reinforce yourself with the armor for extra protection, do so.

Let's pray together and ask God to look at our heart.

Daddy, Abba Father, we come to You now and thank You for being so patient with us. We ask for Your forgiveness as we forgive everyone that has hurt us. We also forgive ourselves for the wrongs we committed knowing that You forgive. Lead us not into temptation, and when we begin to go to that place of our flesh, let us remember that You are faithful and will always make a way of escape for us. We now ask that You would reveal to us the deepest parts of our hearts where we have let invaders or, yes, even demons, play with our emotions. Show us through the Holy Spirit the infections in our hearts that need healing by You, Father. We will not be afraid, but will trust in You, believing that You will make us whole. I understand Father, the phrase no pain, no gain. Just like a physical workout for my temple (body), I also need an emotional and spiritual workout for my heart. I understand that You are about to bring me through some painful deeply rooted heart issues and memories, but the incredible healing I will experience will be worth it. I believe Your word in Romans 8:28 that states that we know that You cause all things to work together for good to those who love You, to those who are called according to Your purpose. I love You, Father, and I trust You to show me the truth and carry me through the journey of healing my heart. Lead me by the hand, in Jesus name. Amen.

Now that the Holy Spirit has our permission to search our heart, we can move forward.

Jesus Sees Through Your Eyes

When you accepted Jesus as your Lord and Savior, He came to abide inside of you. He became the apple of your eye. He now looks through your eyes and sees everything that you have witnessed and experienced. He hears everything you hear. Every man you have looked at and every man's words you have heard. As an example, Jesus saw through your eyes, you looking into the eyes of the man you knew you should not have been with; yet you found yourself yielding every part of your being unto him not knowing if this was your husband. He treated you with respect and even cried with you as he held you in his arms. Then when you looked at him with tears in your eyes, he took advantage of you and kissed you. You thought, *Wow! This feels like the healing I have always wanted.* Or, he may have been the first one who never forced himself on you, so you thought, *He loves me! This has to be love!*

You begin to remember when you shared with him your deepest thoughts and he gazed into your eyes the whole time and listened. He spoke things to you that brought comfort. He told you that he would not treat you as the other men did in the past. He said he would treat you as a woman deserves to be treated. But the loving arms, sweet nothings in your ear, and the kind actions you expected didn't happen as he promised.

*Though his speech is charming, do not believe him, for seven abominations fill his **heart**.*
Proverbs 26:25 (NIV)

Oh, my sister! This is when the pain begins. You gave him everything. You gave away your five senses and your spirit to a man who was not fully committed to you. Whether you had a promise, engagement, or no ring at all; and whether it was casual or premarital sex, it was without your Heavenly Father's permission. The feelings you may have experienced or are experiencing include: betrayal, insecurity, exposure, shame, anger, rage, confusion, being used, as well as many more. Only you know what you are feeling emotionally and spiritually; and the questions you may be asking yourself are:

"My Lord, what have I done?"

"What can I do now?" or

"Is there hope for me?"

Jesus Sees You from His Eyes

Let's look at your experience from Jesus' perspective. He sees your heart, spiritually and naturally. You are the apple of His eye. Not only is He looking from the inside out, but He is also looking from the outside into your heart. He saw and heard it all. The pain you suffered at the idle words and actions of a man or men. You had no security. You exposed yourself, being emotionally *naked* with him. You shared your heart, your emotions, your hopes, your dreams, your past failures, and your fears with him. Sharing made you comfortable, and you believed that since you shared so much of yourself with him, you could trust him with your body, too. First, you were *naked* emotionally, and then you let yourself get naked with him physically.

A Love Letter to the Ladies

Jesus saw you in the vulnerable position with someone you thought was committed to the relationship as much as you were. Unfortunately, a week, a month, or even a year later, after you have committed your physical and emotional self, he chose to "break up" with you. Oh, nooooooo! You realize there was no true commitment and your trust, betrayed. You feel like trash. You feel worthless, used, and abandoned. Your mind starts to wander, and you wonder why you were not good for him or marriage material. You take the blame for his action against you. You were a victim of longing for an earthly husband; when in reality, Jesus, your spiritual husband has been extending His hand to you the whole time.

My sister, there is so much hope for you. If you haven't asked the Lord to forgive you, do so now. You are His daughter, and He sees you as a young, innocent virgin girl. Now, the cycle must stop. What I am going to suggest is something that your normal mind or physical body will try to stop you from doing. You must cut off these hurtful relationships immediately. Please, my dear sister, call on your Heavenly Father. Call on the name of Jesus. Take some time and fall in love with the Savior and Lover of your soul, Jesus.

Take six months to a year to re-evaluate yourself and get to know Jesus more intimately. Don't spend time alone or on the phone with a single (or married) man. The enemy will try to distract you from this quiet time and place the person in your path; either physically or by air waves. Trust me. Most men can tell when a woman is vulnerable, hurting, or emotionally needy, and they will use that to their advantage. They will grab the opportunity when it's presented to them and then leave you. Please note, this is not the case with all men; I am generalizing to make a point.

Pray Psalm 141:4 and make it your deepest commitment of prayer to keep pure for your Bridegroom Jesus.

*Do not incline my **heart** to any evil thing, to practice deeds of wickedness with men who do iniquity; and do not let me eat of their delicacies.*

By inspiration of the Holy Spirit, I wrote the following verse as the Lord was ministering to me about being more aware of guarding my heart.

See, I have been given one heart ... and I am the guarder of this heart. If I just let anyone and everyone in ... wouldn't my heart be crushed by all the trampling feet? And then how will it maintain a healthy heartbeat ... to attract one that Yah (God) has intended for me to meet?

God gave me this personal little poem on how to remember to guard my heart, and now I pray that the Lord would put something on your heart to remind you to do the same. It's so important because when we open our heart to just anyone without any emotional boundaries, we are setting ourselves up for a potentially dangerous situation.

Guard Your Heart

You may wonder how to guard your heart. Well, give it to Jesus. Simple but true. What I mean by this is to be very careful of temptation that may come your way. I will give you a recent example of a situation in my life. There was a beautiful young lady by the name of Jane I met hiking. We seemed to really connect in our conversation and how comfortable we felt to be open with one another. We ended up agreeing to exchange phone numbers and meet up again maybe for a hike as friends, knowing that she was in a relationship. Well, I got a text message from her a few days later. It said, "You won't believe what just happened. I just got in a huge fight and my relationship is over. I would like to talk with you, please." So

I agreed and suggested that we get a bite to eat. Then after a couple of hours of eating, talking about how her relationship ended, and just hanging out, I dropped her off at home.

She then texted me and told me, "I hope this won't make you feel uncomfortable and not want to hang out with me, but I have to confess that I am very attracted to you."

I said, "Thanks for being so open and honest with me. I have to admit that I feel the same way about you."

Then a week later, we decided to go for a hike. After we hiked and I dropped her off at home, she texted me and said, "May I confess something to you?"

I said, "Sure. Of course."

She said, "When we were hiking and when we sat down on the bench, I wanted to kiss you so bad. Do you want to get serious?"

Now keep in mind this was only after two weeks of knowing her, and she had just ended a relationship of three years. So I reminded her again, "I want to take it slow."

She said, "I understand, and I respect that."

Then a couple of days later I texted her and asked, "How are you doing, my beautiful friend?"

She responded back, "Friend?"

I said, "Yes. I told you I wanted to take things slow."

I never heard back from her. My point is, she more than likely was on what people call the rebound. I refused to give in to temptation knowing the painful experiences I have had in the past from making similar poor choices by getting involved with someone on the rebound.

Eternal Intimacy Brings True Harmony

*Above all else, **guard** your **heart**, for everything you do flows from it.*

Proverbs 4:23 (NIV)

*And the peace of God, which transcends all understanding, will **guard** your **hearts** and your minds in Christ Jesus.*

Philippians 4:7 (NIV)

Think of your heart like this: It is a throne hidden behind a door. The throne is beautiful and has elegant decorations and the best pillows for sitting, and it is fit for only One Perfect Person. The fact that I mention *perfect person* should tell you something about who He is, because no one is perfect except for the Person who is also one hundred percent God. That Person is Yeshua (Jesus). He is the King of kings and the Lord of lords. I like to call Him the King of hearts. Your heart and mine. If you try to place anyone else on the throne, you will be deeply disappointed. This is due in part because the door to your heart requires a key that only unconditional love can open. Only Jesus can love you with a pure, unselfish, and unconditional love. Remember, He paid the price for all of the wrongs you committed and those committed against you. Look at this passage from The Message:

Christ arrives right on time to make this happen. He didn't, and doesn't, wait for us to get ready. He presented himself for this sacrificial death when we were far too weak and rebellious to do anything to get ourselves ready. And even if we hadn't been so weak, we wouldn't have known what to do anyway. We can understand someone dying for a person worth dying for, and we can understand how someone good and noble could inspire us to selfless sacrifice. But God put his love on the line for us

by offering his Son in sacrificial death while we were of no use whatever to him.
Romans 5:6-8

Wow! My dear sister, please make sure that you have a lock on the door. In fact, put an alarm on it with a code that only He knows. Don't let anyone or anything that could be considered an idol—boyfriends, girlfriends, family members, etc.—sit on the throne. The place in your heart should be your secret place with Him. Only you and Jesus belong in this room as you spend intimate time with Him on His holy throne of your heart. Remember, Jesus is your Husband and Bridegroom in the Spirit. He calls you His bride right by His side. This room is only for Him, so throw out the impostors as the devil and his demons have no place in your heart or on His throne. Trust Him with the door to your heart, and continue to keep your emotions in check and your thoughts on Him.

Look into Jesus' Eyes

Chapter two discussed your *point of pain*. Now it's time to begin the process of removing every hurt and every person who doesn't belong on His throne in your heart. Give the boot to those people and painful events that should never have been part of your heart in the first place. No longer are you looking into the eyes of the enemy. What the enemy meant for harm, the Lord will heal and use your understanding of Jesus on your throne to set others free. Your greatest pain and healing will be used to help others who will need their own healing. Let's read what the Savior says about the enemy (thief) and his actions toward you:

The thief comes only to steal and kill and destroy; I came that they may have life, and have it abundantly.
John 10:10

Eternal Intimacy Brings True Harmony

The devil tried to use a person(s) or event(s) to steal, kill, and destroy your heart. The thief may have had temporary success, but in the bigger picture, it didn't work. Now, this is the good part. Look what Yeshua (Jesus) said about giving you life in the second part of that verse of John 10:10.

I came that you may have life and have it abundantly.

Jesus didn't come to just give you eternal life but life more abundantly in your relationships, emotional well-being, financial and physical health as well. If you look at the original Hebrew meaning of the word *salvation*, it means not just a *spiritual soul-saving salvation* but a completeness in all areas of your life.

But this is where you must do your part. Now let's look at what the Amplified Bible states in Revelation 3:20 (paraphrased).

Behold, I stand at the door [of your heart] and knock; if you hear and listen to and heed to My voice and open the door [of your heart], I will come in to you and will eat with you, and you [will eat] with Me.

It's time for you to look into the eyes of Jesus. Spend time with Him. Turn off your television, turn off your computer, and turn off your cell phone. Get away from everyone for a moment. Do it now, my sister. Ask Him to forgive you for your sins and your wrongs for prematurely giving your heart, emotions, and body to another man, or woman for that matter. Yes, I am going there. Some readers are or have been in a relationship with another woman. She said to you that she understands you and that only another woman could truly understand you. Repent. Turn from her and ask the Lord to heal you and let Him come into you now.

Call unto the Lover of your soul. Cry out to Him. Be

honest with Him. Some of you may not know what to say to Him. If you are crying, He understands your tears and can hear the expression in your heart even in your tears. Let it flow, my sister. Let the tears and wailing come out. Cry out. Your Father is wrapping His loving arms around you. Feel His safe and comforting arms around you. He doesn't condemn you and doesn't shame you. All is forgiven. Let's look at one of my favorite stories in the Bible . . .

Let me take you back nearly 2,000 years ago to something that Jesus witnessed. A woman was caught in the act of adultery, felt no hope, and was about to be killed. Found in John 8:1–12, this is one the best stories of forgiveness.

> *But Jesus went to the Mount of Olives. Early in the morning He came back into the temple [court], and all the people were coming to Him. He sat down and began teaching them. Now the scribes and Pharisees brought a woman who had been caught in adultery. They made her stand in the center of the court, and they said to Him, "Teacher, this woman has been caught in the very act of adultery. Now in the Law Moses commanded us to stone such women [to death]. So what do You say [to do with her—what is Your sentence]?" They said this to test Him, hoping that they would have grounds for accusing Him. But Jesus stooped down and began writing on the ground with His finger. However, when they persisted in questioning Him, He straightened up and said, "He who is without [any] sin among you, let him be the first to throw a stone at her." Then He stooped down again and started writing on the ground. They listened [to His reply], and they began to go out one by one, starting with the oldest ones, until He was left alone, with the woman [standing there before Him]*

in the center of the court. Straightening up, Jesus said to her, "Woman. Where are they? Did no one condemn you?" She answered, "No one, Lord!" And Jesus said, "I do not condemn you either. Go. From now on sin no more." Once more Jesus addressed the crowd. He said, "I am the Light of the world. He who follows Me will not walk in the darkness, but will have the Light of life."

(AMP)

Notice, Jesus didn't condemn her, but instead He exposed the fact that everyone was a sinner. Who gives other sinners the right to justifiably kill another person for having sinned? After sticking up for the woman, Jesus told her to do one thing: "Go on your way, and from now on, sin no more."

He would not have told her to sin no more if He didn't believe she was not going to fulfill the instruction. Sister, do you know you have the victory over sin and your Father will teach you how to set and keep appropriate boundaries that will keep you from falling into your old natural sinful pleasures? There is always a way of escape. Check out this promise in the Word:

No temptation has overtaken you but such as is common to man; and God is faithful, who will not allow you to be tempted beyond what you are able, but with the temptation will provide the way of escape also, so that you will be able to endure it.

1 Corinthians 10:13

What an awesome promise! Our God is faithful.

Remember, you are His daughter, and His Word states:

But the fruit of the Spirit is love, joy, peace, patience, kindness, goodness, faithfulness, gentleness, and

self-control. Against such things there is no law. Those who belong to Christ Jesus have crucified the sinful nature with its passions and desires. Since we live by the Spirit, let us keep in step with the Spirit. Let us not become conceited, provoking and envying each other.
Galatians 5:22-26 (NIV)

If you notice the last of the nine characteristics of the fruit of the Spirit is self-control. It takes much work, prayer, and a humble heart to practice this on a regular basis. Show Him that you are His by exemplifying the fruit of the Spirit, and there will be no law against you. Crucify your flesh. Yes, the word tells us to crucify our sinful nature with all of its passions and desires. Show others that you are a true disciple of Christ. The root word of disciple is *discipline*. Show the Lord you have self-control. This will not only help you to be blessed but also to be a blessing to your brothers in the Lord as we will discuss in chapter 5.

Eternal Intimacy Brings True Harmony

Chapter Four: Reflections

Take time to reflect on the following questions and scripture reference.

- What is intimacy?
- What part of us does the Bible say we should guard most of all? Why? How do we guard it?

Scripture to meditate on (the Lord's expression of deep intimacy):

To everyone who is victorious I will give some of the manna that has been hidden away in heaven. And I will give to each one a white stone, and on the stone will be engraved a new name that no one understands except the one who receives it.

Revelation 2:17 (NLT)

A Love Letter to the Ladies

CHAPTER FIVE

Whom Are You Trying to Attract?

I believe every person knows deep in their heart when they are making a decision to sin sexually. I am going to be very blunt with you, again. From a man's perspective, I need to tell you that certain things can make it difficult for a man to resist temptation, which makes it easier to lead you into temptation. This book may make some Christians uncomfortable because they may say that as a single man, I have crossed some boundaries in sharing very candid experiences about the *taboo* subjects of modesty and boundaries. These subjects are not taught from the pulpit because they are not easy topics to teach or preach.

It is better for me to take the heat from my critics and know that you, my sister, and your future husband can live a healthy, holy, and prosperous life with one another, than for the enemy to trick you into doing something that you will regret later. Understanding how the enemy operates through men will make you an overcomer. So, here we go.

First, men are easily sexually stimulated. Visual stimulation doesn't require any more than a woman being in a room. Add to that a woman who dresses or handles herself provocatively around a man and he becomes even more stimulated. Let me share with you some profound verses in the Amplified Bible about the power a woman can have over a man. Proverbs 6:24–29 states:

> *To keep you from the evil woman, from the flattery of the tongue of a loose woman. Lust not after her beauty in your **heart**, neither let her capture you with her eyelids. For on account of a harlot a man is brought to a piece of bread, and the adulteress stalks and snares [as with a hook] the precious life [of a man]. Can a man take fire in his bosom and his clothes not be burned? Can one go upon hot coals and his feet not be burned? So he who cohabits with his neighbor's wife [will be tortured with evil consequences and just retribution]; he who touches her shall not be innocent or go unpunished.*

Now, these scripture verses aren't calling you an evil woman, a harlot, or someone who is committing adultery; but if you are offended, some introspection may be in order. Let me remind you, my dear sister, that you are married to Jesus. You are His bride, and He is your Bridegroom. He is a jealous God, so if you place any man on His throne, you are no longer keeping Jesus, your Husband, first.

I would like to point something else out. What about the idea of how not having boundaries and limitations while you are single affects your future husband? How would you feel knowing that the man you are going to marry is making out with someone else? I can only speak for myself, but thinking about my soon-to-be wife kissing another man burns me within. It makes my blood boil with anger and jealousy. It makes me sick to my stomach to think that my wife may be giving certain parts of her body, even if it's only her mouth, lips, and tongue to another man right now.

Some of you may be thinking, *T.J., you are going a little too far now. You are a prude. It is not a sin to kiss someone before you get married.* There are two things to think about; let me just put it to you this way. Warning, I am going to get graphic again. First, have you thought about how many other lips and tongues have been touching his? How many other women has the man you are courting been in contact with, having touched them with his lips and tongue? See? It's a never-ending cycle of not knowing where the lips and tongue of your future husband have been. And you are prematurely kissing someone.

Now, don't get me wrong here. The past is the past. If the man you are courting has made a renewed commitment to the Lord and is practicing full abstinence, then don't hold his past against him. In this case, you may be losing out on the blessing that God has for you.

The second point to consider is this: when you are being prematurely physical in a relationship (kissing, cuddling, making out, even full-on hugs), how do you know that you are not tempting your brother in Christ? Look back at Proverbs 6:27-29:

Can a man take fire in his bosom and his clothes not be burned? Can one go upon hot coals and his feet not be burned? So he who cohabits with his neighbor's wife [will be tortured with evil consequences and just retribution]; he who touches her shall not be innocent or go unpunished.

Wow! This is my interpretation as a single man, beginning in verse twenty-seven: Can a single brother take the passionate fire (the romantic interest he has in an attractive single sister) and have physical interaction with her (kissing, cuddling, long full-body hugs, etc.) and not have his clothes (hormones in his body) be burning with sexual desire?

Continuing with my interpretation, let's look at verse twenty-eight: Can a single brother touch a woman sexually and not have his feet (hormones in his body) be burning with sexual desire?

And finally, verse twenty-nine: So a single brother who plays with sexual temptation with his neighbor's (future) wife [will be tortured with evil consequences and just retribution]; the single brother who sexually touches his single sister (someone's future wife) shall not be innocent or go unpunished.

Okay, you may be thinking, *What about the grace and forgiveness of God?* Well, of course God forgives us of all sin. But what a shame if we use the fact that we can ask for forgiveness from Him as an excuse to keep sinning because we don't want to give up our fleshly desires.

> *Well then, should we keep on sinning so that God can show us more and more of his wonderful grace? Of course not! Since we have died to sin, how can we continue to live in it?*
>
> Romans 6:1-2 (NLT)

As you can see, I was very up-front with you because you as a sister should know how challenging and tempting it is for a single brother in the Lord at times. We need you to be straightforward about your boundaries. Now, I don't want to put this all on you. As single brothers in the Lord, we also need to take the initiative to be the gentlemen that our Father expects us to be toward you, His daughters.

A Love Letter to the Ladies

So, let's look at the following scripture from the perspective as if you are already spiritually married to your future husband:

> *For the wife does not have [exclusive] authority and control over her own body, but the husband [has his rights]; likewise also the husband does not have [exclusive] authority and control over his body, but the wife [has her rights].*
>
> 1 Corinthians 7:4 (AMP)

So again, your body is reserved for him, and his body is reserved for you. Keep it that way. You don't have to be married or the man you are courting doesn't have to be married to be committing adultery. Let's read what Jesus says about our heart and adultery:

> *You have heard that it was said, "YOU SHALL NOT COMMIT ADULTERY;" but I say to you that everyone who looks at a woman with lust for her has already committed adultery with her in his heart. If your right eye makes you stumble, tear it out and throw it from you; for it is better for you to lose one of the parts of your body, than for your whole body to be thrown into hell. If your right hand makes you stumble, cut it off and throw it from you; for it is better for you to lose one of the parts of your body, than for your whole body to go into hell.*
>
> Matthew 5:27-30

Now, Sister, I am being blunt as usual because there have been too many of my single sisters and brothers hurt due to the lack of knowledge. If you or the man you are dating are engaging in anything that may lead to either of you feeling sexually aroused, you need to stop immediately. In fact, you should not put yourself in a tempting situation. So use wisdom. Always ask yourself this question: "Would I bring Jesus with me into this situation?"

Whom Are You Trying to Attract?

This question may help keep you in check and keep you from hitting the deck and getting into another emotional wreck!

Physical boundaries need to be discussed up-front within a romantic relationship. Withholding that information is not fair to your boyfriend or fiancé. Here's a simple example of how to communicate your boundaries with one another: "Babe, (or "Honey," or "Sweetie pie," whatever the term of endearment), I just want to let you know that I am comfortable giving you a frontal hug, but only for a few seconds at a time, in order to avoid any temptation."

Now, that may seem cheesy or unusual to say at first, but follow up the statement with, "You know I deeply care about you and am attracted to you, so I don't want to lead you into temptation because that would be unfair to you. I know you feel the same way. So that you know, you may kiss my hand or my cheek, but to avoid temptation, I'd rather you not kiss me on the lips or on my neck until the pastor says to you, 'You may now kiss the bride.' I know you are a man who loves God and me and will respect my boundaries, as I will do the same."

The interesting thing about using this approach, my sister, is that if he disrespects you or tries to go beyond your boundaries, it is a clear indication of a man who you may not want to continue to court. It is an indicator that he does not respect you and has his own selfish agenda in mind. I'm not trying to be cruel or unforgiving; I'm just giving you something to seriously think about.

It's about being real and respecting yourself and him. It is a win-win situation for you, my sister. Think about it. If this man is to be your husband, he will prove his love for you. Remember what was discussed in chapter one: 1 Corinthians 13—love is patient. If you end up separating because he is not the man for you, both you and he will have respected each other. The great thing is not only did you bless each other, but also both of your future spouses will be blessed because you both chose to keep yourselves pure by not prematurely giving any part of your physical body to each other.

God will honor both of you for waiting and in turn, will reward each of you on your respective wedding day and honeymoon night. Make the man who seeks to earn your love wait. He will recognize first that you are the daughter of the Most High Father and second that you are someone's future wife. He will recognize that he is better off not kissing someone else's wife. At the same time, I also don't recommend long full-frontal hugs, long times of cuddling, or giving each other a massage—all which can easily lead to heavy petting and other forms of fornication.

So, my sister, keep your guard up, and remember that your body is the Lord's first and your future husband's second. You can do it, my sister. Do it with the strength of the One who lives in you. So call upon the Holy Spirit who lives within you, and let Him be greater within you than the tempter who is in the world.

You are from God, little children, and have overcome them; because greater is He who is in you than he who is in the world.

1 John 4:4

Dress Appropriately for the Beautiful Woman You Are

The way a woman carries and presents herself in her dress and appearance is a very touchy subject for many women. If the church would approach this subject with love and sincerity, like it truly deserves, then it wouldn't be such a taboo subject. I pray that you will just have an open heart and mind to what I write.

Whom Are You Trying to Attract?

Let me preface this section by mentioning that single, engaged, and married men have shared their honest hearts with me about how a woman dresses. It is an inevitable conversation. But please give me a moment to share this with you. I promise it will bless you and your future husband. Just as importantly, this will bless your brothers in the Lord. First, let's look at a couple of scriptures. Let's start with 1 Thessalonians 5:22 in the King James Version:

Abstain from all appearance of evil.

And the other scripture:

I also want women to dress modestly, with decency and propriety, not with braided hair or gold or pearls or expensive clothes, but with good deeds, appropriate for women who profess to worship God.

1 Timothy 2:9-10 (NIV)

Now, please, if you believe this verse is saying that a woman shouldn't dress nicely, fix her hair, wear makeup or earrings, then you are not looking at the intent behind this scripture. The heart or spirit of this scripture is this: if the man is focused more on the outward appearance of how you look than the inward woman that God created you to be, then you are heading for a major lifelong disappointment. Look at this scripture:

Charm is deceptive, and beauty is fleeting; but a woman who fears the LORD is to be praised.

Proverbs 31:30 (NIV)

Physical beauty is fleeting. It passes away. If the man you are trying to attract is caught up in your physical beauty, then he is more likely caught up in the spirit of lust. And he is going to be highly disappointed the day things begin to get wrinkly and saggy. Sorry, Sister, just being real.

A Love Letter to the Ladies

So what kind of man are you trying to attract? A man who uses his fleshly eyes to find a wife, or a man who is using God's eyes to find a wife? Ideally, you want a man who is looking beyond your obvious physical beauty and is interested in the internal and eternal qualities that you have been gifted with. Your spirit, personality, intelligence, wit, selflessness, passion for Jesus, passion for those without a relationship with Jesus, or what many men look for and say, "Wow! She is great with children. What an honor it would be to have her be the mother of my children."

Yes, my dear sisters. A man you want is a man who sees the characteristics that will last for a lifetime. Let me bring some balance here, though. Yes, a man wants a woman who takes care of herself and her body, and treats her body like it is his. Here's God's Word:

> *In this same way, husbands ought to love their wives as their own bodies. He who loves his wife loves himself. After all, no one ever hated his own body, but he feeds and cares for it, just as Christ does the church — for we are members of his body.*
>
> Ephesians 5:28-30 (NIV)

First, I want to share with you one of many stories that I have about my single brothers in the Lord and their confessions about you, women, the most amazing beautiful creatures that God has ever created. This is a true story about a single brother in the Lord whom I'll randomly call Tony. That is not his real name. One day, he was sharing with me his frustrations about trying to keep what Job 31:1 states:

> *I made a covenant with my eyes not to look with lust at a young woman.*
>
> (NLT)

Whom Are You Trying to Attract?

    This brother in the Lord was someone who had made a full commitment to the Lord and was sharing with me his honest, heartfelt difficulties of trying his best to keep his eyes pure before the Lord. Remember what Jesus said about adultery in Matthew 5:27-30 that it is better to lose a body part than to be thrown into hell.

    So this brother was explaining to me how a sister in the Lord that he cares about tends to wear tight jeans or pants. He understands she is not showing any skin, but she is still showing the *image* of her body with its curves and shape. He continued, explaining that this sister was exposing parts of her cleavage when she wore low-cut blouses or shirts. He said the fact that he could see the *details* of her glutei maximi (butt), hips, thighs, and yes, even near her private area, the inner thighs, in the tight jeans she wore was enough to bring him into a serious temptation to lust.

    Sister, I'm sure you have been driving down the road and noticed on the back of a car or truck a silhouette or shadow image of a nude woman. The portrayal encourages the lustful and sexual desires of a man, leading him to look at a woman exclusively as a sexual object.

    Notice, I didn't even go there about the poolside or the beach. Now you may say, "Who do you think you are to judge me on what I wear?"

    You may call me Mr. Super Religious, but I have to be blunt and take the chance of being criticized. It is more important for me to let you know about the struggle that most of my brothers in the Lord encounter when our sisters don't leave *anything for the imagination* without any concern. By the way, when I say don't leave *anything for the imagination*, I don't mean our brothers have the right to sin and lustfully fantasize about a woman.

For example, a sister is wearing a nice summer dress or business attire that is not tight-fitting, and the man says to himself, "Hmmm, I wonder how she would look in tight jeans or in a bikini."

No! What I am saying is at least he has the opportunity to stop himself from a tempting thought. It's better for him to start with a less-tempting situation, instead of starting with the tight jeans or bikini image, in which he will certainly be tempted and may think, "How would she look in her panties and bra or (even worse) nude?"

Yep, I am laying it all out there. I have had enough. I am absolutely tired of hearing my brothers sharing with me their heart-wrenching stories of the conflict they are in. I have personally experienced what they have shared with me, and I want to look at my sisters with absolute purity of heart, too. As brothers in the Lord, we are trying our best to fulfill the scripture verses in 1 Timothy 5:1–2:

Treat younger men as brothers, older women as mothers, and younger women as sisters, with absolute purity.

(NIV)

It devastates me to see how we as the church of Christ have allowed the devil to creep the secular media's ideas into our lives/church to teach our daughters how to attract a man. In fact, I am enraged at the success of the devil. I'll never forget the time when I decided to catch the local news for a moment, which I rarely do. All of a sudden, there was a quick advertisement for the upcoming story the station was going to share after the commercial break. This is exactly what it said and showed on the television:

"Hey, ladies, don't go away! We are going to show you how to give your behind a little extra appeal to catch his eyes!" And they showed a lady in tight jeans shaking her behind.

Whom Are You Trying to Attract?

You may be thinking, *Whoa! What you saw was harmless. T.J., you and your brothers just need to get delivered from the spirit or demon of lust.* Come on now, Sister. I am just simply going to say this: "Help a brother out!"

I understand some of you didn't have a mother who was a positive example for you, or you are trying to fit in with the modern-day culture. You may be dressing the same way you saw your mother dress. Or perhaps you are just trying to fit in with your peers and friends to look attractive, which in reality is borderline provocative. Also, another reason you may dress that way is some of you may not be able to afford a new wardrobe. But the Lord will provide.

When we truly want something, we all get creative in getting what we want. A great example of this is when I see a woman wearing tight jeans but at the same time being modest by wearing a long-enough blouse that covers her buttock area. Guess what? She still looks great and attractive. Please, I just ask you to seriously consider taking this subject to prayer. I have a responsibility to the Lord to share this with you, so my conscience is clear. Most importantly, remember your value; you are the daughter of the Most High Father.

As you can see, my sister, I am just stating this out in the open because it needs to be said. Some of you may not even realize that you are making it more challenging for your brother to not lust. Let me put it to you in the form of a question. What type of man are you trying to attract?

A man who judges a woman based on what she can physically offer? Or a man who is forced to see beyond the obvious modestly portrayed beauty and see you as God sees you? Make him see your inner person, your heart, soul, feelings, mind, intelligence, dreams, hopes, and feminine side. These are the sensitive yet very strong and passionate qualities of a human being that every man is trying to get more in touch with. The incredibly amazing beauty that is inside of you may be missing from a man. This is the mysterious and creative part of you that we as men are always trying to get closer to and learn more about.

The point is not for you to follow some legalistic set of rules but for you to check the motives of your heart. When you are dressing and look at yourself in the mirror do you think, *Oh, yeah, I will get his attention now!* or *I know I look good in these jeans, and they make men turn their heads!* or *It's alright, I'm not showing too much skin on top; it's okay to show a little.* If you have any of these thoughts, my sister, you need to seek the Lord regarding this issue, because you should never do anything that will lead your brother or anyone to sin. Don't use the beauty God blessed you with as a tool to tempt others to sin. I selected certain parts of Ezekiel 16:7–15 for you to meditate on:

> *You grew up and became a beautiful jewel. Your breasts became full ... And when I passed by again, I saw that you were old enough for love. So I wrapped my cloak around you to cover your nakedness and declared my marriage vows. I made a covenant with you, says the Sovereign Lord, and you became mine. And so you were adorned with gold and silver. Your clothes were made of fine linen and costly fabric and were beautifully embroidered. And you became more beautiful than ever. You looked like a queen, and so you were! Your fame soon spread throughout the world because of your beauty. I dressed you in my splendor and perfected your beauty, says the Sovereign Lord. But you thought your*

Whom Are You Trying to Attract?

fame and beauty were your own. Your beauty was theirs for the asking.

(NLT)

Find balance regarding the issue of dressing modestly. I believe if you will truly seek the Lord about dressing appropriately, He will direct you so you look beautiful and you will glorify Him.

The woman who knows how to be attractive without compromising her image is the woman who will attract strong brothers in Jesus. She doesn't feel she needs to be showcasing the incredible outer shell that her Creator has blessed her with in order to get a man's attention. From a man's viewpoint: make the man work hard for your attention, affection, admiration, and acceptance. You are worth more than any amount of power, money, or influence a man can have. The best description of the type of woman who is after God's heart and a man hopes to find is found in Proverbs 31:10-31:

A wife of noble character who can find? She is worth far more than rubies.
Her husband has full confidence in her and lacks nothing of value.
She brings him good, not harm, all the days of her life.
She selects wool and flax and works with eager hands.
She is like the merchant ships, bringing her food from afar.
She gets up while it is still dark; she provides food for her family and portions for her servant girls.
She considers a field and buys it; out of her earnings she plants a vineyard.
She sets about her work vigorously; her arms are strong for her tasks. She sees that her trading is profitable, and her lamp does not go out at night.
In her hand she holds the distaff and grasps the spindle with her fingers. She opens her arms to the poor and extends her hands to the needy.

A Love Letter to the Ladies

When it snows, she has no fear for her household; for all of them are clothed in scarlet.
She makes coverings for her bed; she is clothed in fine linen and purple. Her husband is respected at the city gate, where he takes his seat among the elders of the land.
She makes linen garments and sells them, and supplies the merchants with sashes.
She is clothed with strength and dignity; she can laugh at the days to come.
She speaks with wisdom, and faithful instruction is on her tongue.
She watches over the affairs of her household and does not eat the bread of idleness.
Her children arise and call her blessed; her husband also, and he praises her:
Many women do noble things, but you surpass them all. Charm is deceptive, and beauty is fleeting; but a woman who fears the LORD is to be praised.
Give her the reward she has earned, and let her works bring her praise at the city gate.

(NIV)

Overcome evil with good by helping a brother out. There are enough temptations in this world as it is. Be greater by the One who lives in you, rather than being part of the tempter (Satan) who is in the world. The renewing of the way you present yourself in your appearance and also the chastity of your body is just the beginning. Let's get back to talking about the heart in the next chapter. When we discuss the heart, this will expose the emotional, mental, intellectual, and spiritual connection we have with others and how to be cautious of being too *naked* with someone who isn't your husband.

Whom Are You Trying to Attract?

A Love Letter to the Ladies

Chapter Five: Reflections

Take time to reflect on the following questions and scripture reference.

- Why should we have physical boundaries in romantic relationships?
- Why does it matter what I wear or how I dress? Doesn't God see my heart? He really doesn't care about how modest I appear in the way I dress, right?

Scripture to meditate on:

Charm is deceitful and beauty is passing, but a woman who fears the Lord, she shall be praised.

Proverbs 31:3 (NKJV)

CHAPTER SIX

It Starts with the Heart

My sisters, it is now time to talk about the heart. This is the part of our being that is so precious. What I mean by precious is mostly everything we do is motivated by our heart, or in other words our passion and desire. The Word of God discusses the imperativeness of being very cautious with our heart. But first, let me discuss what *guards* or *protects* the heart, which is the ribcage. What is so fascinating is how both the heart and ribcage seem to be dependent on one another yet still have separate functions. The word *rib* is first discussed in the Bible in Genesis 2:18-22:

> *Then the Lord God said, "It is not good for the man to be alone. I will make a helper who is just right for him." So the Lord God formed from the ground all the wild animals and all the birds of the sky. He brought them to the man to see what he would call them, and the man chose a name for each one. He gave names to all the livestock, all the birds of the sky, and all the wild animals. But still there was no helper just right for him.*

It Starts with the Heart

So the Lord God caused the man to fall into a deep sleep. While the man slept, the Lord God took out one of the man's ribs and closed up the opening. Then the Lord God made a woman from the rib, and he brought her to the man.

(NIV)

My sisters, I'm going to talk later about a man's heart, which intricately involves the *rib*. Of course his woman (helpmate) was formed from his rib. But anyway, there is something I want to point out here about the rib. I believe the Holy Spirit revealed something to me as I was meditating on His Word. Just imagine this idea that my Father showed me, my dear sister.

There is a Spiritual Rib

When a man is missing his ribcage, how can he feel fully protected? The structure guards his heart and lungs. The heart and lungs are obviously very sensitive vital organs. God created the ribs to protect these parts of our body.

Symbolically, the rib is a spiritual shield of protection for the heart and lungs in a human body. It gives us some amazing insight into how a man and woman relate to one another. The heart is where the issues of life affect our emotions. For example, when a man's heart is not guarded, he is exposed and more vulnerable to emotional and spiritual attacks. When his life issues and emotions are not guarded, there will be no peace in his heart.

When a man's heart is affected due to the lack of his *peaceful rib* being in the *right* place, his lungs are exposed, and his breath is taken away. So, ladies, you as the rib have a kind of power that can take a man's breath away. You may know the feeling yourselves, when a man looks you straight in the eyes and makes you feel like you are the most beautiful and only woman on the earth. That is the power of the heart, and it shows how our emotions are affected by healthy or unhealthy actions and words of others. Check out this verse in the Bible:

*An anxious **heart** weighs a man down, but a kind word cheers him up.*

Proverbs 12:25 (NIV)

Let's look at Proverbs 14:30 from different versions of the Bible. The reason I am doing this is because each version adds something valuable to the point I am making. By doing so, you will have a better understanding of how important it is for you, as the rib, to guard your own heart so you can then help guard your brother and future husband's heart.

A heart at peace gives life to the body, but envy rots the bones.

(NIV)

A peaceful heart leads to a healthy body; jealousy is like cancer in the bones.

(NLT)

A sound mind makes for a robust body, but runaway emotions corrode the bones.

(The Message)

A tranquil heart is life to the body, But passion is rottenness to the bones.

(NASB)

This is my favorite version …

A calm and undisturbed mind and heart are the life and health of the body, but envy, jealousy, and wrath are like rottenness of the bones.

(AMP)

It Starts with the Heart

First, let's look at these two scriptures:

The heart of her husband safely trusts her; So he will have no lack of gain. She does him good and not evil All the days of her life.
Proverbs 31:11-12 (NKJV)

Also look at this scripture:

Guard your heart above all else, for it determines the course of your life.
Proverbs 4:23 (NLT)

Words Affect the Heart

Words are powerful. Remember, God created the earth and everything in it by speaking words. When negative words or words of affirmation are spoken over someone's heart, it will either tempt the heart to be anxious or to be in good cheer. When someone is giving a person quality time or no time, it still speaks to that person's heart. Your nonverbal communication, your glance, eyes, smile, facial expressions, body language, etc. all speak without saying a word.

A cheerful look brings joy to the heart, and good news gives health to the bones.
Proverbs 15:30 (NIV)

This is true whether we are talking about the man's heart that you are making an effort to capture or your own heart that you are giving away. When someone speaks words, remember life and death are in the power of the tongue, and those who love its fruit eat it. So if you are speaking words of life to a man, you are speaking encouragement. In contrast, if you are speaking words of death to a man, you are speaking discouragement. That is why the Word of God warns us to be very wise with our words because of the way it affects our heart.

The Heart Needs Love

We all want to be in love. This is normal. Translating the word *love* from the Greek text in the Bible, we find that there are different types of *love*. First, *agape* is known as unconditional love. Unconditional love is the act of being concerned about the other person's highest good regardless of the personal benefits or gain we get from it. It is a selfless love.

Phileo love translated from the Greek language means to approve of, like, treat kindly, welcome, and befriend. It is a brotherly friendship and conditional love. Think of it this way: if you do this for me, then I will do that for you. You scratch my back; I'll scratch yours. It shouldn't be *tit for tat*, but unfortunately many people think this way.

Then there is the word for erotic love, *eros*. Translated, it describes a love between people who are married. This is a very passionate, romantic love where both people have a deep yearning or desire to express sensuality to one another. In our American culture, we tend to get *eros* love confused as the deepest love, which is *agape*. We are obsessed with *eros* love. There is nothing wrong with erotic love, because God created us to desire it. In fact, the Song of Solomon, a book in the Bible, is dedicated to this type of powerful and intoxicating love. Of course, we as single Christians look forward to experiencing this to its fullest in marriage.

Now there is nothing wrong with longing for all three types of love. We just need to understand, my dear sister, that God has already given us the deepest part of love. *Agape* was fulfilled by the sacrifice of His only begotten Son, Jesus. There is nothing we could do to pay for our own sins, so He paid the price that we couldn't pay. That was an incredible selfless act of love toward us. It is the greatest act of *agape* love ever.

When Jesus died on the cross for each of us, we received His grace (undeserved mercy or favor). In return, we should want to do our best to show our love to Him. How do we do that? Give Him your life as a living sacrifice. This was discussed in chapter one. Being a living sacrifice fulfills not only *agape* love, but also *phileo* love. Jesus described love best in John 15:12-15:

> *This is My commandment, that you love one another, just as I have loved you. Greater love has no one than this, that one lay down his life for his friends. You are My friends if you do what I command you. No longer do I call you slaves, for the slave does not know what his master is doing; but I have called you friends, for all things that I have heard from My Father, I have made known to you.*

Verse thirteen describes *agape* love: l*aying down your life for your friends.*

Then verse fourteen mentions *phileo* love: y*ou are my friends if you do what I command you.*

I propose that we learn of His *agape* love first, followed by *phileo*, or conditional love, next. Once we have learned these two types of love and can live them daily, we are better prepared for the appropriate physical boundaries expressed by *eros* love. With *eros*, there are no limitations as it applies to a man and woman once they are married. Now that we understand the three major types of love, we can continue to discuss things of the heart and interacting with the opposite sex.

Protect the Heart

When we first meet someone, we tend to be on our *best behavior*. It is true that the first impression is a lasting one, but we need to be cautious and protect our heart. To start, we need to ask ourselves, "How do I safely determine how much and how fast to share my emotional, intellectual, and spiritual intimacy with someone?"

Of course, you want to express yourself honestly and share your heart's dreams and goals to determine if you are a match with the person. But, to love someone else, you must first learn to guard your heart so you can safely capture someone else's. Allow me to use myself as an example of what not to do.

I met a lady whom I found very attractive. I will use the name Hannah for anonymity purposes. When I first met her, I noticed she had a ring on her finger, so I asked, "Are you married?"

She answered, "No."

I then asked, "Are you engaged?"

Again, she said, "No."

Wanting to know more about the ring, I questioned, "Promise ring?"

She said, "Yeah, something like that."

As we conversed, she mentioned that she and her boyfriend had been together for four years. I asked, "What is he waiting for?"

She said, "I don't know, but I'm not going to wait much longer."

Then she smiled at me.

So, I began to keep both of them in my prayers. About two weeks later, we were talking again. I wanted to share some of my life experiences in order to help her out with her situation, so I asked her if her boyfriend would feel comfortable if we exchanged numbers and talked sometime. She told me it didn't matter, because things were not working out between them. We smiled at each other and exchanged phone numbers.

It Starts with the Heart

Another couple of weeks passed, and during that time frame, we briefly talked on the phone and sent a few text messages to each other. About the same time, we agreed to have dinner together. We had a great time. Up to that point, I was under the impression that she and her boyfriend had broken things off. Come to find out, they had just broken things off a few days prior to our meeting for dinner. Our friendship flourished, and she started to open up to me. She admitted the man was verbally abusive to her and she was concerned about her own safety at times.

We spent a lot of time with each other. The problem was not that we were spending time together; it was the fact that ninety-five percent of that time, we were alone. It set us up to be too emotionally and spiritually intimate with one another within the short period of two weeks. Fortunately, the only physical interaction we had was holding hands when we prayed together and giving each other a hug when we said goodbye. Don't be deceived. Those brief and *innocent* physical connections of holding hands when praying and those brief, warm hugs spoke volumes within my soul.

What was developing deep within my own soul (my mind, will, and emotions) was something called a soul tie, but I didn't know it at the time. My personal definition of a soul tie: two people who become deeply connected by the intertwining of their physical, spiritual, and emotional beings, which creates a deep level of intimacy. Our intimacy began very early in the relationship. By the third day of spending time alone with each other, we were deeply connected, or so I thought.

Wanting to be honest with Hannah, I shared my romantic feelings for her on the third visit. She had a suspicion about my feelings toward her and told me she didn't know how she felt about us. I told her I was willing to wait, and she responded by saying it wasn't fair to me to wait. Smiling, I shared with her it was my free-will choice to wait, and left for the day.

I was excited about our conversation and thought that she would eventually decide to pursue a courtship with me. In my excitement, I shared with mutual friends about what I thought would happen. Others overheard the conversation with my friends and told her what I said. She confronted me and unfortunately, the friendship ended on a bad note. She took offense and thought I was telling my friends that we were already in a committed relationship. I explained to her that was not true, but it was too late as she had made up her mind to end our friendship. She did admit that is was emotionally painful for her as it was for me to break off our friendship. The good thing that came from this was at least we didn't get into a deeper relationship that would have been primarily based off the rush of being too emotionally and spiritually intimate with each other too quickly.

Initially, when we were spending time with each other, my intentions were to lead her into a deeper relationship with Jesus so she would be healed of her past relationship. As a result, spending time with Hannah led me to become emotionally and spiritually connected to her. As you can see, this decision was clearly a mistake, even if my intentions were good. Therefore, my sisters, I highly recommend when you know a man is emotionally vulnerable that you refer him to a brother in the Lord and/or a member of the pastoral staff to help him be healed in Jesus. Do it for yourself and for his heart. Jesus will honor you for that.

Looking back, I know I should have used wisdom knowing Hannah had recently broken off the relationship with a man she had been with for four years. I let my emotions and spirit become tied to someone who really wasn't healed of the past relationship or ready for a new one. Our desires to love and be loved can get the best of us. Lessons learned.

My first lesson: don't try to counsel someone whom I find attractive both physically and personally. As she opened up to me, I felt comfortable to share with her about my past, my values, future goals, etc. The fact that she trusted me and I trusted her made it easier for both of us to become emotionally vulnerable, thus opening our hearts too quickly to one another.

Another lesson: don't put myself in a situation with a woman who is on the rebound. By *rebound* I mean: with the ending of one relationship, finding solace and healing through another relationship. In my case, Hannah was experiencing her own personal time of emotional healing. The last thing she needed to do was get involved in another emotional relationship with another man. She needed a sister in the Lord to lead her to Jesus for her healing. It may sound complicated, but that's when praying and communicating with your Father in heaven and reading the scriptures are important. Also, having an older woman to keep you accountable is necessary to help you avoid any unnecessary emotional hurt and pain. Titus 2:3-5 states:

> *Older women likewise are to be reverent in their behavior, not malicious gossips nor enslaved to much wine, teaching what is good, so that they may encourage the young women to love their husbands, to love their children, to be sensible, pure, workers at home, kind, being subject to their own husbands, so that the Word of God will not be dishonored.*

Let me share a powerful story about a woman who has an encounter with Jesus at Jacob's well. She was thirsty for natural water but found out there is something deeper than quenching your fleshly thirst.

A Love Letter to the Ladies

...*So Jesus, being wearied from His journey, was sitting thus by the well. It was about the sixth hour. There came a woman of Samaria to draw water. Jesus said to her, "Give Me a drink." For His disciples had gone away into the city to buy food.*

Therefore the Samaritan woman said to Him, "How is it that You, being a Jew, ask me for a drink since I am a Samaritan woman?" (For Jews have no dealings with Samaritans.)

Jesus answered and said to her, "If you knew the gift of God, and who it is who says to you, 'Give Me a drink,' you would have asked Him, and He would have given you living water."

She said to Him, "Sir, You have nothing to draw with and the well is deep; where then do You get that living water? You are not greater than our father Jacob, are You, who gave us the well, and drank of it himself and his sons and his cattle?"

Jesus answered and said to her, "Everyone who drinks of this water will thirst again; but whoever drinks of the water that I will give him shall never thirst; but the water that I will give him will become in him a well of water springing up to eternal life."

The woman said to Him, "Sir, give me this water, so I will not be thirsty nor come all the way here to draw."

He said to her, "Go, call your husband and come here."

The woman answered and said, "I have no husband."

Jesus said to her, "You have correctly said, 'I have no husband'; for you have had five husbands, and the one whom you now have is not your husband; this you have said truly."

The woman said to Him, "Sir, I perceive that You are

a prophet... I know that Messiah is coming (He who is called Christ); when that One comes, He will declare all things to us."

Jesus said to her, "I who speak to you am He." At this point His disciples came, and they were amazed that He had been speaking with a woman, yet no one said, "What do You seek?" or "Why do You speak with her?"

So the woman left her waterpot, and went into the city and said to the men, "Come, see a man who told me all the things that I have done; is this not the Christ, is it?"

John 4:6-19, 25-29

I believe many women and men, while reflecting on their past failed relationships, may have had the following thoughts.

I have been unsuccessful at many relationships. I have tried my best to be the person that I thought would be desirable. I gave my time, energy, heart (issues of life), hopes, and dreams into those past relationships, but they still failed! Will I ever figure this out?

Imagine how the Samaritan woman felt. She had been married five times, and the man she was with wasn't even her husband. The story tells us that she tried five times to be fulfilled as a wife, but it didn't work. We can surmise that there were some serious, deep-rooted issues in her heart, which probably stemmed from early childhood experiences. Of course, I believe that the conflicts with each husband, which led to divorce, weren't all her fault. But, after the fifth unsuccessful marriage, one would hope she would begin to think to herself, *Maybe there is something I am doing in my life that needs to be changed in order for me to have a successful marriage.*

She was on track to start the same cycle over again with this sixth man. Just imagine the rejection, self-blame, self-hate, and worthlessness she may have been feeling after being divorced five times. You may have heard that the definition of insanity is doing the same thing over and over again and expecting a different result. The good news: Jesus was at the well to minister to her.

Listen to how Gary Chapman in his book *The Five Love Languages* describes what he calls the *in love experience* and how leading with our emotions can be very deceptive. Although he is discussing this in the context of a marriage, I believe it applies to any romantic relationship. Let's read what he writes.

> The "in love experience" temporarily meets one's emotional need for love. It gives us the feeling that someone cares, that someone admires us and appreciates us. Our emotions soar with the thought that another person sees us as number one, that he or she is willing to devote time and energies exclusively to our relationship. For a brief period, however long it lasts, our emotional need for love is met. Our tank is full; we can conquer the world. Nothing is impossible. For many individuals, it is the first time they have ever lived with a full emotional tank, and it is euphoric.
>
> In time, however, we come down from that natural high back to the real world. If our spouse has learned to speak our primary love language, our need for love will continue to be satisfied. If on the other hand, he or she does not speak our love language, our tank will slowly drain, and we will no longer feel loved. Meeting that need in one's spouse is definitely a choice. If I learn the emotional love language of my spouse and speak it frequently, she will continue to feel loved. When she comes down from the obsession of the "in love experience," she will continue to be filled. However, if I have not learned her primary love language or have

chosen not to speak it, when she descends from the emotional high, she will have the natural yearnings of unmet emotional need. After some years of living with an empty love tank, she will likely "fall in love" with someone else and the cycle will begin again.

My dear sister, there are two things I want to point out. First, when Gary says *after some years of living with an empty love tank*, that statement can apply to any romantic relationship even if the relationship only lasted a few weeks or months. Secondly, the lady at the well was in the self-defeating cycle that Gary referred to as the *in love experience*. She was thirsty for the love that only true love would quench.

Now you may be wondering, *What does the story of the woman at the well have to do with me? And Gary Chapman is talking to married people! I haven't even been married yet, so obviously I haven't been divorced yet.*

Hold on a minute. Remember this scripture:

Do you not know that your bodies are members of Christ himself? Shall I then take the members of Christ and unite them with a prostitute? Never! Do you not know that he who unites himself with a prostitute is one with her in body? For it is said, "The two will become one flesh."
1 Corinthians 6:15-16 (NIV)

When you have sex with someone who is not your husband, you still become one flesh with him (physically connected), and therefore united with him emotionally and spiritually. You must be aware of this and go to Jesus for your healing from these relationships. The Message version of the Bible states it well in 1 Corinthians 6:16-20:

There's more to sex than mere skin on skin. Sex is as much spiritual mystery as physical fact. As written in scripture, "The two become one." Since we want to become spiritually one with the Master, we must not pursue the kind of sex that avoids commitment and intimacy, leaving us more lonely than ever—the kind of sex that can never "become one." There is a sense in which sexual sins are different from all others. In sexual sin we violate the sacredness of our own bodies, these bodies that were made for God-given and God-modeled love, for "becoming one" with another. Or didn't you realize that your body is a sacred place, the place of the Holy Spirit? Don't you see that you can't live however you please, squandering what God paid such a high price for? The physical part of you is not some piece of property belonging to the spiritual part of you. God owns the whole works. So let people see God in and through your body.

When we feel deprived from certain healthy human needs, we will do what it takes to fulfill those empty, dry, or *thirsty* places. Unfortunately, when we are *needy*, we end up getting involved in a relationship or relationships that may compromise our values in order to meet those *needs*. Let me introduce a simple idea known as the ***Amazing A's***. They are the emotional, relational, physical, and psychological needs that ultimately come from our Almighty Father.

Meet the Amazing A's

The ***Amazing A's*** include: ***Attachment, Affection, Acceptance, Attention, Admiration, Appreciation,*** and ***Affirmation.*** Now for all human beings, physical life begins when a baby is conceived. When we grow, we are automatically protected by our mother's womb. We are connected or ***attached*** by the umbilical cord to our mother. Wherever she goes … we go. Whatever she eats … we eat.

Whatever she hears ... we hear. Whenever she feels pain, we know it. We are *attached*. As a full-term baby, we are in the womb for nine months. Now if there was ever an example of all of us being attached to someone, there it is. From the beginning of our life process, we are attached to our mother.

We have a natural human desire and need to be attached to somebody. So let's look at the word attach in *Merriam-Webster Dictionary*.

One definition: to bind by personal ties (as of affection or sympathy)

Another definition: to make fast (as by tying or gluing)

The first definition from *Merriam-Webster Dictionary* uses the word *affection*. This is another **A** word that we will review along with the word *attachment*. Let's break down the word *attachment* or *attach* from God's Word.

Using *Strong's Concordance of the Bible*, let's look up the word *attached*. *Attached* is used in the New King James Version for the first time in Genesis 29:34. The word *attached* in English means *joined* and in Hebrew, *lavah*. *Lavah* means the following when its definition is further translated:

1) to join, be joined a) (Qal) to join, be joined, attend b) (Niphal) to join oneself to, be joined unto

Furthermore, *Gesenius's Lexicon* defines it as:

to adhere, to be joined closely to anyone

Interestingly enough, this verse refers to when Leah was trying to win the ***affection*** or ***attachment*** of her husband Jacob, because he loved her younger sister Rachel. Let me give you some background on the story about Jacob, Leah, and Rachel. Jacob saw and fell in love with Rachel. He made an agreement to work seven years to earn the honor of Laban, Rachel's father,

A Love Letter to the Ladies

in turn for her hand in marriage. After working the seven years, Laban gave Rachel to Jacob. He was excited to consummate the marriage according to the promise made by Laban. That evening, it was dark, and Jacob assumed he was consummating the marriage with Rachel. When morning came, who was lying next to him in bed? Rachel's older sister, Leah! He was fooled! He ended up working another seven years so he could be with Rachel. Jacob loved Rachel more than Leah, and the Lord knew this, so the Lord had compassion on Leah, and she gave birth to many sons, while Rachel was barren. Genesis 29:34 states:

> *She conceived again and bore a son and said, "Now this time my husband will become attached to me, because I have borne him three sons." Therefore he was named Levi.*

Understand that Leah's attachment had nothing to do with the physicality of sex. She obviously was sexually active with Jacob, thus birthing a third son. The problem for Leah was she knew Jacob wasn't attached to her emotionally. He loved Rachel more than her, and it ate away at Leah's soul. In this case, Leah competed with Rachel. It is not God's will for a woman to compete with another woman to gain a man's affection. In the Garden of Eden, it was one man with one woman.

Competing for the *attachment* and *affection* of a man will tear you and the other woman apart. Look back at the verse where Leah begins her sentence with,

"Now *this time* …"

This shows that she tried at least two other times previously to win Jacob's *affection* and *attachment* through childbirth. She probably tried winning his heart by other means as well. Maybe she tried to cook better meals and took time to ensure the house was extra clean. Or … some of you may not like what I am about to say here, but maybe she would make advances to persuade Jacob to have sex with her more often and would do things in the bedroom that he enjoyed to win his ***affection*** and ***attachment***.

My goodness, Sister! If you ever base who you are on the way a man is giving or not giving you ***attachment*** or ***affection***, you need to get a grip on yourself. Get yourself in order and know that true intimacy is found in your relationship with God first. Remember, you are valuable.

Who can find a virtuous wife? For her worth is far above rubies.

Proverbs 31:10 (NKJV)

Now, let's look at the definition of ***affection*** in *Merriam-Webster Dictionary*:

1: a moderate feeling or emotion

2: tender attachment: <u>FONDNESS</u>.

Surprise, surprise! The definition of ***affection*** includes the word ***attachment***. A moderate feeling or emotion is also a component of the definition. Sometimes our feelings and emotions can challenge us as individuals. Leah desired ***affection*** from her husband Jacob and was constantly competing for it, while the woman at the well had been searching for it. Think about it. The Samaritan woman sought her ***attachment*** and ***affection*** with her previous five husbands and didn't find it. She searched again for the sixth time with a man who wasn't even her husband.

Let's look at the *A* word, ***acceptance***. Referring back to the story of the woman at the well, in John 4:9-10 when Jesus asked her to give Him a drink of water, she responded, "How is it that you, being a Jew, ask me for a drink since I am a Samaritan woman?"

It was culturally inappropriate for a Jew to communicate with a Samaritan. First, she was in shock that He spoke to her in the first place. Then, she was surprised when He asked her to give Him something and He accepted it. This part of the analogy highlights how we can behave with the Lord.

We may have been impatient by rushing into relationships because we just wanted to be accepted and feel loved. When we do that and the relationships don't work out, the pain of its ending may harden our hearts. Then as a result, it may be hard to accept true and pure intimate love from our Lord. Remember, it is normal to want acceptance, but we must ensure the acceptance is healthy and from someone who has our best interests at heart.

This is a good place to look at another *Amazing A: attention*. Let's look specifically at the third definition in *Merriam-Webster Dictionary*. It states:

3a: an act of civility or courtesy especially in courtship <she welcomed his attentions>

3b: sympathetic consideration of the needs and wants of others: ATTENTIVENESS

Wow! See, every person—especially a normal, healthy woman like you—wants someone to have the *sympathetic consideration of your needs and wants* without any ulterior motives. From childhood to adulthood, we are *hardwired* to want some attention. It is natural for us to want others to be sympathetic toward us and show us general courtesies.

Another significant *A* word is **admiration**. *Merriam-Webster Dictionary* defines it as:

It Starts with the Heart

1: archaic: WONDER

2: an object of esteem

3: delighted or astonished approbation

All excellent definitions. The third definition uses the word *approbation*. With further investigation, the word *approbation* lead me to two other words—*commendation* and *praise*. *Commendation* simply means *compliment*. Now, I know without a doubt, every woman, young lady and girl loves to be an object of esteem, to be given a compliment with delight and astonishment. There is nothing wrong for a woman's physical beauty to be appreciated by others. But more importantly, a woman should be admired for her inward beauty (personality, intellect, wit, spirit, kindness, and genuineness). Therefore, ***admiration*** is definitely an *A* word every lady should hear from others who truly care for her.

Next, ***appreciation*** is a wonderful *A* word I have learned that ladies, well ... truly appreciate. Again using my favorite dictionary, *Merriam-Webster*, let's focus on the first part of the definition, which states:

1 a: a feeling of expression of admiration, approval or gratitude

It's interesting that within the definition of ***appreciation***, ***admiration*** is used, and it is also an ***Amazing A*** word. The approval or gratitude explanation is one that everyone appreciates. We are grateful when an individual says "Thank you" and shows their appreciation toward us. I have learned over the years that when I say "Thank you" and "I appreciate you" to any of my family members, especially my mother and sisters, it really brings a smile onto their face. To feel appreciated makes a person feel respected and shows that you don't take them or their time for granted. When a young girl is helping her dad or mom with little chores around the house, and her parents acknowledge her by saying "Thank you," it builds her confidence. So please remember, my sister, it is normal for you to desire to feel appreciated.

The last *A* word for us to understand is ***affirmation***. The root word of ***affirmation*** is *affirm*. *Merriam-Webster Dictionary* gives the following definitions:

1 a: VALIDATE, CONFIRM

b: to state positively <he *affirmed* his innocence>

2: to assert (as a judgment or decree) as valid or confirmed

3: to express dedication to

When we feel validated, or someone assures us of their love, or as the third definition states, *to express dedication to*—we can trust the person, and it gives us peace. From my many years of being single and having many sisters in the Lord share with me their relationship struggles and emotional needs, I have come to some of the following conclusions. This is where most girls, who didn't have a father or at least a father figure affirm his unconditional love, may have been seriously emotionally and/or psychologically devastated. It is very important to a woman that she has peace in knowing that a man is dedicated to her. A girl who has a father figure who was regularly in her life in a healthy way learns this. She knows that she can always rely on him to express his affirmation, dedication, commitment, etc. to her by showing her some of the ***Amazing A's: attachment, affection, acceptance, attention, admiration,*** and ***appreciation*** in a nonsexual way.

In my conversations with Christian women I asked them the following question: "What are the top five qualities you desire in a man?" Most of them stated at least one of the three following qualities: loyalty, honesty, or integrity. These are words containing traits of ***affirmation***. Therefore, based on my conversations, it is my opinion that a woman desires and needs to receive this trait, which I believe encompasses all seven ***Amazing A's*** that have been discussed.

As you can clearly see, a girl truly needs these ***A's*** or attributes not only from her mother, but from her father as well. If any or a combination of these ***Amazing A's*** are seriously lacking in a woman's life as she develops, beginning with prenatal development, through infancy, toddlerhood and childhood through adolescence. By the time she reaches early adulthood, she may be in for some considerable challenges.

When you become a young adult, you are expected to know how to form intimate relationships and to become aware of what a truly healthy love is. That has to be very difficult to do if throughout your childhood you were not experiencing any of these attributes with people around you, again, especially from your father. Therefore, be careful not to prematurely cross boundaries with a man because you are desperate to fulfill an emotional need. Let me share a story about a young lady who had a challenging time relating to men appropriately due to her father being killed at the age of two.

I met Tassah at my workplace. She was a young lady, and her actions in the workplace implied she wanted attention from men and received it. She was very attractive and dressed moderately provocatively: tight jeans, low-cut blouses, thick lipstick; and she was very flirtatious. She sat next to me. I remember talking to her about Jesus and always trying to encourage her to get to know Him. We ended up building a good professional relationship and soon got to know each other outside work as well. From our conversations, I surmised that she was constantly in and out of relationships. I recognized she was trying to seek and find the true water of love that would quench her soul.

At one point when she was single, she began to get a little more flirtatious with me, but it felt like she may have just wanted to test my waters, if you will. I ignored her flirtations, knowing she needed to fall in love with Jesus first and allow Him to heal her before she could have a relationship with me – or anyone, for that matter. One day, she asked me if I ever wanted to get married.

I said, "Of course I do."

She said, "Yeah, I really want to get married."

I recall bluntly asking her if she believed the reason she was in and out of relationships with men and felt a desperate need to have a man in her life was because of her not having a father growing up.

She stated, "Well, I have thought of that before … maybe."

I did my best to encourage her to go to church with me and learn about Jesus and His Father, but she always declined.

I began decreasing the time we spent together until the friendship faded away. After I had not connected with her for a few months, the Lord put her on my heart. The Holy Spirit began to tell me that the man she was currently with did not have her best interests at heart. Now, I hadn't spoken to her in a while, and the last time we spoke, she wasn't in a relationship. I was not looking forward to telling her that the Lord told me the man she was with did not have her best interests at heart and argued a little with the Lord about it. But arguing with Him is a waste of time. So, I sent her a text message saying hello. After she responded, I sent her a text message and shared what the Lord told me to tell her. She replied with shock and texted,

"How did you know I was in a relationship?"

I told her that God told me. She texted me that she was interested in hearing what I had to say and would call me in an hour. Speaking with her on the phone made me feel like she was expecting me to tell her that I would be the better choice for her. That may be speculation on my part, but I sensed it from her while we were on the phone. I told her this, "The Lord says, 'In order for you to be ready for a healthy, God-centered romantic relationship, you must first fall in love with Me and come to know Me as your Father through intimate fellowship with My Son Jesus.'"

Then I told her that if she continued to go down the road she was on, she would forever be disappointed and would never quench the thirst in her soul. Believe me, my dear sisters, being direct with her was not easy.

Both women – the one at the well and my friend Tassah – needed their emotional needs met. This chapter first discussed man's heart and how a woman is the *rib* that guards it. This includes guarding your own heart as well. Remember what Proverbs 4:23 states:

> *Keep and guard your heart with all vigilance and above all that you guard, for out of it flow the springs of life.*
> (AMP)

Remember if your body is your future husband's body, and your heart is in your body, and your issues of life and the emotions attached to them are in your heart, then that means your body, heart, issues of life, and emotions are not only your own but are for your future husband, too. Your heart, having been affected by past relationships, including those with your ex-boyfriends and ex-fiancés, can seriously affect your relationship with your future husband.

A Love Letter to the Ladies

The issues of life deal with emotions, and if any of the *Amazing A's* were absent in your life, especially throughout your childhood, it's time to receive those attributes from your Heavenly Father. Receive the ***Attachment, Affection, Acceptance, Attention, Admiration, Appreciation*** and ***Affirmation*** from Jesus before you consider a future romantic relationship with a man. These attributes form what is referred to as our identity, which will be discussed in the next chapter. Boy, or maybe I should say, Girl, am I excited to share with you what the Word of God says about our identity and the process I experienced in the search for my own identity in the Father.

It Starts with the Heart

A Love Letter to the Ladies

Chapter Six: Reflections

Take time to reflect on the following questions and scripture reference.

- What are the Amazing A's?
- What Amazing A's did you receive in the past and the present? Which ones did you not receive or do you feel you are currently lacking?

Scripture to meditate on:

"I have loved you even as the Father has loved me. Remain in my love. When you obey my commandments, you remain in my love, just as I obey my Father's commandments and remain in his love."
John 15:9-10

CHAPTER SEVEN

Know Your True Identity

As a woman, do you base your identity on how you were treated in your past relationships? Do you determine your worth based on being a good mother or on your desire to have children? How about on what society or the media defines as a successful woman? What about the influence of how your parents raised you and what their expectations of you were? How about this one: "If I get a good, God-fearing man who will treat me right and give me the respect that I have always desired and deserve as a daughter of the Most High Father, I will have my true identity?" Well, I have some bad news for you. Even though it is a very good thing to desire a husband who is a godly man, if you are basing your identity on your relationship with him, you are in for a rude awakening. No other person determines your identity.

The best example of identity is the story of Jesus' identity as the Son of God being tested by Satan. Matthew 4:1-11 states:

Then Jesus was led up by the Spirit into the wilderness

to be tempted by the devil. And after He had fasted forty days and forty nights, He then became hungry. And the tempter came and said to Him, "If You are the Son of God, command that these stones become bread."

But He answered and said, "It is written, 'MAN SHALL NOT LIVE ON BREAD ALONE, BUT ON EVERY WORD THAT PROCEEDS OUT OF THE MOUTH OF GOD.'"

Then the devil took Him into the holy city and had Him stand on the pinnacle of the temple, and said to Him, "If You are the Son of God, throw Yourself down; for it is written, 'HE WILL COMMAND HIS ANGELS CONCERNING YOU'; and 'ON their HANDS THEY WILL BEAR YOU UP, SO THAT YOU WILL NOT STRIKE YOUR FOOT AGAINST A STONE.'"

Jesus said to him, "On the other hand, it is written, 'YOU SHALL NOT PUT THE LORD YOUR GOD TO THE TEST.'"

Again, the devil took Him to a very high mountain and showed Him all the kingdoms of the world and their glory; and he said to Him, "All these things I will give You, if You fall down and worship me."

Then Jesus said to him, "Go, Satan! For it is written, 'YOU SHALL WORSHIP THE LORD YOUR GOD, AND SERVE HIM ONLY.'" Then the devil left Him; and behold, angels came and began to minister to Him.

Look at verse two.

And after He had fasted forty days and forty nights, He then became hungry.

The devil came to Jesus after He had been fasting from food for forty days and forty nights. The devil came to tempt Him when He was *weak*. If the devil will tempt the King of kings and the Lord of lords with an imitation of what the Father had in store, he will tempt you, too.

Imagine if you were *fasting*, neglected, or missing one or all of the ***Amazing A's*** in your life. One way the devil works to steal your identity is found in the following example: you have longed for attention and admiration from your father or a father figure all your life. All of a sudden, a nice-looking, friendly man who seems to have your best interests in mind comes into your life. You get close to him. It looks like he knows exactly what you need, and he gives you all the attention and admiration you want. You end up trusting him to the point where you give up your physical boundaries, and before you know it, fornication (premarital sex) happens. A couple of weeks later, he leaves you. The devil sent an imitation.

Look at verse three.

And the tempter came and said to Him, "If You are the Son of God, command that these stones become bread."

Well, there the devil goes using the word *if*. He is trying to attack the identity of Jesus by putting doubt in His head. The devil wants Jesus to prove that He is the Son of God. At the end of Matthew chapter 3, just before Jesus had this encounter with Satan, John baptized Him in water. Matthew 3:16-17 states:

And Jesus when he was baptized, went up straightway from the water: and lo, the heavens were opened unto him, and he saw the Spirit of God descending as a dove, and coming upon him; and lo, a voice out of the heavens, saying, This is my beloved Son, in whom I am well pleased.

(ASV)

You see, His Father blessed Jesus by telling Him who He

was, the Son of God; then the devil came to tempt Him by trying to make Him doubt His position as the Most High Child of His Heavenly Father.

    I believe one of the most important family relationships a person can have is their relationship with their earthly father. Your earthly father should do his best to reflect your Heavenly Father. It is especially important during one's childhood and teenage years. The fact is, many do not have a good relationship with their father. Let me address the relationship of a father to his daughter from my perspective.

    How a father expresses his love to his daughter will give her an idea of how she is to be loved. This expression can be either negative or positive, but I will focus only on the positive. When a father respects, honors, guides, provides, protects, and yes, tells his daughter that she is his beautiful little girl, her value is established. The encouraging comments will build a healthy foundation. She will be directed to a genuine, healthy, and true explanation of her value, not only as a young girl, teenager, and young lady, but also as a woman for the rest of her life.

    Ideally, the father spoke and interacted with his daughter positively so that she transitioned from childhood into adolescence and learned that her lasting value is based on internal qualities, not physical characteristics. Sister, it is easy for a teenage girl to believe in the false idea that they are in a beauty pageant in everyday life due to the influence of the media and peer pressure. If a young lady's value is based on the idea that they have to be the most beautiful one of all, they are in for a long, winding maze of confusion, hopelessness, emptiness, and deception. For this reason, it is important for every woman to understand her identity from a young age.

    Knowing one's identity is imperative for men, too. Let me share some personal moments that shaped my life at an early age. When I was four, my parents divorced, and my dad was completely out of my life. With my father absent during my childhood, I had no example of a Godly father. This made life growing up as a boy very difficult. I was always looking for acceptance and affirmation from a father figure. I also was seeking for a male influence in my life that I could look up to.

When I was eight years old, my grandmother and grandfather kicked my mom, my sister, and me out of their house because my mom's new boyfriend was black. We had to live on our own. Those were tough times. It was a very difficult time for me, because the only male figure I had at that time was my grandfather. Although he wasn't the best male influence or good example of a father figure, being forced out of his home still made me feel rejected. The emotional impact it had on me still was very significant because I no longer had any communication with my grandfather.

One time, we were out of electricity and low on food because the welfare check had not arrived as scheduled. We hardly had any food on the table. I remember promising my mother that when I got older I would provide all the food for us, and I would take care of her. Of course, I now understand that it is not the child's responsibility to provide for the parents, but my childlike heart saw the pain my mom was enduring while feeling like a failure because she was unable to provide for my little sister and me.

The pain was overwhelming for my mother. Just imagine looking at your little babies knowing that all you had to feed them was ramen noodles and cheap hotdogs. After a while, my mother was sick and tired of ramen noodles and hotdogs, but my sister and I never complained. In fact, we smiled and looked at her with thanks in our eyes as we chowed down the dogs. By the way, I now hate ramen noodles with its MSG and definitely won't eat a specific brand of hotdog again.

Oh, the pain my mama must have felt, yet at the same time, the love and hope she must have had knowing that she had her babies there with her. She spoke life over me regularly.

Let me a share a couple memories that had a positive impact on my life. They both involve my uncles. First, a special moment I shared with my uncle Ricardo.

He said, "Come here, Mijo. Let's go outside in the backyard and play!"

He took me outside and my mama, grandpa and grandma were already in the backyard.

He said, "Look over there!" as he pointed. I saw it … a brown and orange toy Jeep! I was amazed, in shock, and so excited! I ran toward it.

"Is this mine?" I asked.

"Yes!" He said. "Come on now, I'll help you get in it."

I remember trying to step into it. It was hard to get in, so he picked me up and placed me in the Jeep. I remember my legs were too short to reach the pedals to make the car move. Then my uncle said, "Mijo, put your feet up, and I will push you."

He pushed me around the backyard so fast. It was so fun! Everyone was watching. I heard my grandma say, "Ricardo, be careful. Slow down!"

He responded, "He's alright!"

My mom was smiling and laughing as she watched me having a blast. I was giggling and laughing, too. Boy, was that fun! Then we stopped.

As I was laughing, he picked me up and gave me a big hug, rubbed the top of my head, kissed me on the cheek, and said, "I love you, Mijo."

Yep, he was one who showed me true unconditional love from a male's perspective and gave me an understanding of a father's love for his son.

Then there is my uncle Jody. I remember when he died; I was about three years old. I was devastated, as he was another male figure in my life who showed me unconditional love.

One fond memory about my uncle Jody comes from my mom speaking positively into me by telling me, "Don't worry, uncle Jody left you all of his brains."

She would say that because my uncle Ricardo would always call me Chewbacca because of my big head. So my mother would encourage me by saying, "Mijo, your head is big because your uncle Jody left behind his brains for you. And you are real smart and are going to get good grades in school, and many kids will wish they had a big head like you!"

I know as I share these stories, some of you have never experienced unconditional love from your father. You may not have had a dad in your life because he left you and your mother at a young age. Or, maybe he died when you were young, like my friend Tassah's dad did when she was only two years old. Perhaps your dad simply was an absent father who only paid your mom child support, but never spent time with you in person or on the phone. It could be any reason, but your dad wasn't there for you.

I understand. Go ahead and cry. You have the right. It can be painful. But, I have some good news for you. There is a Father for you. And this Father sees your tears and received them from the angels because you are so precious to Him. When you don't have words to say because you are hurting so badly and all you can do is cry, don't you worry about it. Our Father knows what is on our hearts and minds and considers your tears as prayers to Him. Revelation 8:4 states:

Know Your True Identity

And the smoke of the incense, with the prayers of the saints, went up before God out of the angel's hand.

Now, you may be thinking to yourself, *How does He know my prayers if I only cried with tears and didn't speak one word?* Remember, Adam was alone in the Garden of Eden, and the Lord knew his heart's desires and blessed him with a wife without Adam having to ask Him. Jesus in Matthew 6:8 states:

So do not be like them; for your Father knows what you need before you ask Him.

This scripture doesn't mean you don't ever have to say actual words when you pray; God looks at the heart. The quality and sincerity of your prayers is what truly matters. Sometimes I don't know what to pray, so I cry with tears unto the Lord. Hallelu-Yah! Sister, He will never forsake you or leave you. He is the One who keeps His eyes on you. We all need a Daddy. The Heavenly Father will embrace you as you deserve to be embraced. A wonderful scripture, which I have paraphrased to make it more personal and intimate, is Psalm 27:10:

When my father and my mother forsake and abandon me, then YOU my Heavenly Father, adopt me, take me up and embrace me in YOUR loving arms.

As I wrote this book, I cried and laughed all the way through. Sometimes there is pleasure in pain. It's best explained this way: When the Father saw His Son suffering on the cross, He had to look beyond the temporary pain of what was happening to His begotten Son and see the everlasting pleasure He would have with Him and with His countless adopted sons and daughters. What an amazing Father. And Brother (Jesus), for that matter. The love of the Daddy and Son, our Father and

Brother, is absolutely incredible! Read this scripture from The Message Bible:

> *How blessed is God! And what a blessing he is! He's the Father of our Master, Jesus Christ, and takes us to the high places of blessing in him. Long before he laid down earth's foundations, he had us in mind, had settled on us as the focus of his love, to be made whole and holy by his love. Long, long ago he decided to adopt us into his family through Jesus Christ. (What pleasure he took in planning this!) He wanted us to enter into the celebration of his lavish gift-giving by the hand of his beloved Son.*
>
> Ephesians 1:3-6

He loves you. Show your love for Him. Let Him in.

> *Here I AM standing at the door (of your heart), knocking. If you hear My voice and open the door (of your heart), I will come in to you and eat with you, and you will eat with Me.*
>
> Revelation 3:20 (Paraphrased)

As you come into a deeper personal relationship with Him, you will naturally learn more about Him as He teaches you to live the *love life* that is in His Word, the Bible, and written as His holy commandments. He will reveal Himself and His love unto you.

> *Whoever has My commands and keeps them is the one who loves Me, and the one who loves Me will be loved by My Father, and I will love you and reveal Myself to you.*
>
> John 14:21 (Paraphrased)

Now let's look at John 10:9-13:

> *I am the door; if anyone enters through Me, he will be saved, and will go in and out and find pasture. The thief*

comes only to steal and kill and destroy; I came that they may have life, and have it abundantly. I am the good shepherd; the good shepherd lays down His life for the sheep. He who is a hired hand, and not a shepherd, who is not the owner of the sheep, sees the wolf coming, and leaves the sheep and flees, and the wolf snatches them and scatters them. He flees because he is a hired hand and is not concerned about the sheep.

So what I believe the Lord is saying here is He is the Door of the sheep; if you come through Him, you will be saved to live with Him forever. Not only that, you will come in and out of His secret place with Him and find the love, joy, and peace that you have so longed for. Your mama, papa, grandma, grandpa, uncle, aunt, guardian, etc. are not the True Shepherd; they are hired hands, and you, represented by the sheep, aren't truly theirs. Your hired hand sees the wolf, which is the devil and his demons, working through your boyfriend or girlfriend, who will use you until they get bored with you and leave you. Unfortunately, they can't fully protect you or can't fully heal you from the wolf, and you may look at this as if they are abandoning you (one of His sheep).

In other words, they are to take care of you, but you can't expect them to be the perfect Shepherd (Leader). There is only one True Shepherd: Jesus. He is your true and perfect Leader, Lover, Father, and King of your heart.

Your Identity is in His Unconditional Love

Once you know true love and *who* you are loved by, then your identity is secure. You have no need to search for your identity any longer as you know His unconditional love is personally directed to you. The New American Standard Version states the word *love* for the first time in Genesis 22:2. This scripture is not talking about a romantic, erotic love between a man and woman. It is talking about the love a father has for his child. The Lord God Almighty loves you as His own daughter. Look at the following story about Abraham and Isaac, which exemplifies Abraham's trust in his Heavenly Father. The story is an example to us about how to love and trust our Heavenly Father, too.

The story in Genesis chapter 22 consists of Abraham being tested by God. God told him to take his only son, whom he loved, and sacrifice him as a burnt offering. When Isaac realized that there was no animal with them to sacrifice, he asked his father Abraham about it. Abraham in faith told his son that God Himself would provide the offering. So Abraham tied up his son on the mountain with wood on the altar and began to lift the knife to sacrifice him, but God sent His angel to tell him not to harm the boy. He then told Abraham that there is a ram to sacrifice, and Abraham called that place "The Lord will provide." Then God made the following promise to Abraham for putting his trust in Him in Genesis 22:15-18:

> *The angel of the LORD called to Abraham from heaven a second time and said, "I swear by myself, declares the LORD, that because you have done this and have not withheld your son, your only son, I will surely bless you and make your descendants as numerous as the stars in the sky and as the sand on the seashore. Your descendants will take possession of the cities of their enemies, and through your offspring all nations on earth will be blessed, because you have obeyed me."*

(NIV)

When you read the original Hebrew origin of the story, you'll see that Isaac was not a five to ten-year-old boy whom Abraham could forcefully tie down to make him be a sacrifice. He was a mature and strong young man who loved his father so much he trusted his father's words that God would provide for Himself a sacrificial lamb. Isaac laid himself voluntarily down on the altar. He was proving his love to his father by trusting his dad's comment, which was spoken in faith. Abraham was proving his love to his Heavenly Father by trusting God's Word. That is some incredible trust and love.

> *By faith Abraham, when God tested him, offered Isaac as a sacrifice. He who had embraced the promises was about to sacrifice his one and only son, even though God had said to him, "It is through Isaac that your offspring will be reckoned." Abraham reasoned that God could even raise the dead, and so in a manner of speaking he did receive Isaac back from death.*
>
> Hebrews 11:17-19 (NIV)

Let me give you a more modern-day example. Your father is in the swimming pool with his arms wide open telling you to jump. You have never jumped into a pool before and you are afraid. Your daddy is telling you not to worry because you will be safe when he catches you. You think to yourself, *Well, my daddy always protects me, provides for me, loves me, and won't let me get hurt.*

You take a deep breath, bend your knees a bit, and take a big leap of *faith* and trust him. Your father catches you. You are in his arms laughing and he gives you a big kiss on the cheek and says, "Good jump, my girl!"

God tested Abraham to determine if he would be willing to put his only son to death. The obedience was the act that led to the covenant between God and Abraham. Read Genesis chapter 17. Abraham's action left a great impression on his son Isaac about trusting and loving God. Because Isaac saw his father's faith in God to provide a sacrifice for them, it made sense that Isaac would trust his father's judgment and advice on how to find a wife. Isaac trusted his earthly father to find a woman (Rebekah) who would become a good wife for Isaac. Abraham wanted his son to be blessed with a woman who was from their blood line, because she would be a lady who shared the same faith in God. Abraham sent his servant and gave him a common sign of how he knew if she would be a good woman for his son. One of the main factors would be she would not only offer water to his servant, but also to all of his camels, without any hesitation. Rebekah was a hardworking woman of the Lord. Read the full story of Rebekah in Genesis 24.

Abraham trusted God, and Isaac trusted Abraham. The same concept goes for you, too, my sister. You should be able to trust both your Heavenly Father and biological father. How your earthly father treated you will help give you discernment that was discussed earlier. For example, if you had a good earthly father who showed you love and gave you the ***Amazing A's*** like attention, affection, admiration, affirmation, etc., then you know what to look for in a man. Unfortunately, some of you may not have had a loving father and wonder how to know if a man is good for you. Use the wisdom of God's Word to help you judge a good man from one who is a wolf in sheep's clothing.

Along with wisdom and discernment, get plugged into a loving *church* that has older sisters who can mentor and assist you in the second-most-important decision you will make in your life, which is whom you choose to marry. Consider a woman who is older, both spiritually and in actual age. If she is married, be sure the husband is a man who walks with the Lord. Think of him as a spiritual father to you. You should be able to trust and speak confidentially to them. They can hold you accountable. Also, meet with your pastor and his wife to get feedback about the relationship with your suitor. No matter how old you are, my sister: nineteen, thirty-nine, or fifty-nine, don't feel ashamed or intimidated to ask for help. The purpose of the body of Christ is to offer guidance and counsel.

I want to share an incredible revelation that He gave to me through a vision. This vision shows us the amazing love that the Father expresses to us both as His children in a family and as individuals. Remember our identity is based alone on His unconditional love for us. We must fall in love with our Father, His Son, and the Holy Spirit before we can fully love anyone else, especially our future spouse.

God Gave me a Vision

I saw the walls of oppression and depression crumbling and the children of Zion crying tears of happiness. I saw the pits of pride and selfishness become empty and the children of Zion dancing with leaps of joy. I saw the chains of addiction and procrastination being broken and the children of Zion running with feet of freedom. I saw the lies of deception and premarital conception exposed and the children of Zion speaking truth with tongues of praise.

In the Spirit, I saw the Father waiting with open arms as the children of Zion were crying due to isolation, rejection, and abandonment. Those who were afraid of receiving love or loving someone were now in His arms, and He was healing every emotional void as they embraced Him and looked into His face.

It was the simplicity of love from our Father above that brought wholeness. I saw His children holding hands in a full circle, as they surrounded something or someone. It was a large figure, and as I looked closer, I saw the most beautiful vision in my life … it was the largest leg in the universe. It was the leg of our Heavenly Father. Children were holding hands, and

A Love Letter to the Ladies

grasping and embracing their Father, just as a child would do when their father walked in the door just arriving home from work. They were embracing Him with love, excitement, gratitude, freedom, and adoration, and were looking up into His face as He looked down at each one and gently put His hand on each one's face and head.

He loved them with a love that compared to no other. Each one was given the individual attention and love they so longed for from their Father. Yet there was no favoritism shown to any of the children. It was incredible. No one was jealous of the love the Father had for each child. No one felt rejected, abandoned, alone, left behind, or less important than any other one gathered around Him.

The Father began to sing a love song to His children. They looked into His eyes ... and listened to His voice. Oh my, His voice! It was the Voice of voices, the most precious Voice of all. The song was simple, "You are My son. You are My daughter. And I AM Your Father."

And he continued, "You are My son. You are My daughter. And I AM Your Father."

Tears were flowing from my eyes as I saw the vision and heard the song. Then His children from every single nation sang back to Him a simple song of adoration. "We are Your sons. We are Your daughters. And You are our Father." And they continued, "We are Your sons. We are Your daughters. And You are our Father."

This was the purest concept of unconditional love that I have experienced. As I looked closer, I saw that His Son Yeshua (Jesus) was leading the way in a group hug. Then He said in the vision, "Now you know, My children, the fullness of the love of My Father and why I had to die and rise from the dead.

I loved you with a love so you could be with Me forever with My Father above. He is a Father of absolute relentless love! Remember, My children, My heartfelt prayer in John 17. It was for you."

My sisters, I implore you to take a moment right now and look up John chapter 17 and read it. You will see how beautiful Yeshua's prayer is and how it even includes all of us believers who are currently living on earth.

I shared that vision with you to show how imperative it is to be healed from all relational pains you have had in your past. Remember how your identity is based on your personal relationship and the value our Heavenly Father has placed on you. He paid the highest price by sending His own Son Jesus to suffer a very painful death for you. Your healing makes you whole and allows your identity to never be questioned again.

My sister, do you know His intimate love? If not, come to Him now and be healed. It's as if Jesus is saying to you with open arms, "Come as you are and let your Father; Brother Jesus; and the Lover of your soul, the Holy Spirit sanctify you." Strong's Concordance gives the following definition for the word *sanctify*:

    1) to render or acknowledge to be venerable or hallow
    2) to separate from profane things and dedicate to God
        a) consecrate things to God
        b) dedicate people to God
    3) to purify
        a) to cleanse externally
        b) to purify by expiation: free from the guilt of sin
        c) to purify internally by renewing of the soul

Will you allow Him to bring healing to the deepest part of your soul? Are you hungry enough for Him to make you holy like He is holy? You need to get desperate for Him. Remember that this is a process. Sanctification is not a quick-fix solution. It takes time. Allow the Holy Spirit to do His work, but you must cooperate with Him by doing your part in yielding your will to Him.

Words Have Power

Some of you may be familiar with secular rap artists who use the slang phrase "Call me your daddy" while rapping in their songs. Don't call someone your daddy just because his rap songs say he is your daddy. In reality, those men who say, "Call me your daddy" are *prophe-lying* to you. P*rophe-lying* means speaking words over someone that are not true. It's the opposite of prophesying, which speaks the truth over you. When someone speaks anything over you, always check to see if it lines up with the Bible. If it does, make sure that you have peace in your heart and mind before you make a serious decision to follow the advice or listen to what is spoken. A prophesy usually will confirm something that you already know; or, it can be used to bring you to the next level toward your destiny. The key is to not try to force or manipulate the prophecy to happen but to continue to pray that God's perfect will be done.

There is partial truth when *men* rudely say, "Who's your daddy?" or "I'm your daddy." What I mean by partial truth is that many of these men in your past were being led not by our Heavenly Father but by their *fleshly* father the devil. They, just like the devil, are always focused on their own selfish desires. Yeshua exposed the truth when He spoke that there are only two fathers. One who is the true Father, and the other, who is the false father. To learn more on what Yeshua said about this subject, read John 8:12-28.

Know Your True Identity

So, my sister, which father are you going to trust? Consider who has been lying to you and who has been telling you the truth. Which father has been stealing from you, and which one has been giving you everything you need? Who has disowned and used you, and who has adopted and loved you? You need to make a choice. Read these scriptures on what Jesus states about Himself and the Father and being one with them:

> *"If you had known Me, you would have known My Father also; from now on you know Him, and have seen Him."*
>
> *Philip said to Him, "Lord, show us the Father, and it is enough for us."*
>
> *Jesus said to him, "Have I been so long with you, and yet you have not come to know Me, Philip? He who has seen Me has seen the Father; how can you say, 'Show us the Father'?*
>
> *"Do you not believe that I am in the Father, and the Father is in Me … "Believe Me that I am in the Father and the Father is in Me; otherwise believe because of the works themselves.*
>
> John 14:8-11
>
> *"I will ask the Father, and He will give you another Helper, that He may be with you forever; that is the Spirit of truth, whom the world cannot receive, because it does not see Him or know Him, but you know Him because He abides with you and will be in you.*
>
> *"I will not leave you as orphans; I will come to you.*
>
> *"After a little while the world will no longer see Me, but you will see Me; because I live, you will live also.*
>
> *"In that day you will know that I am in My Father, and you in Me, and I in you. "He who has My commandments and keeps them is the one who loves Me; and he who*

loves Me will be loved by My Father, and I will love him and will disclose Myself to him"
John 14:16-21

My sister, which father are you going to disown? Come to Jesus and ask Him to forgive you for being in the false father's (your boyfriend's, fiancé's, ex-boyfriend's, ex-fiancé's) arms. Let Him know you are sorry for listening to the lies of the devil and you are now reaching out to your True Father. Come and run to Him as a little girl does when she sees her daddy returning home from a long road trip. Don't be afraid to embrace Him in full totality. He will give you the love you have been longing for.

My sisters, now that we have addressed the first type of love and the need of healing to know your true identity, I would like to transition back to the second time the word *love* is used in the Bible, which is in Genesis 24. This time it refers to the love between a man and woman.

*Then Isaac brought her into his mother Sarah's tent, and he took Rebekah, and she became his wife, and he **loved** her; thus Isaac was comforted after his mother's death.*
Genesis 24:67

One of God's most beautiful gifts is that of marriage. The first marriage relationship in history was between Adam and Eve. In order for you to have a healthy, future romantic relationship and marriage, you must understand who you are in the Lord and who you are as a woman. When you are comfortable as the woman God created you to be, then He can begin the next chapter in your life, which may include a husband. Therefore, don't lose hope; and remember the scripture Galatians 6:9:

And let us not lose heart and grow weary and faint in acting nobly and doing right, for in due time and at the appointed season we shall reap, if we do not loosen and relax our courage and faint.

(AMP)

A Love Letter to the Ladies

Chapter Seven: Reflections

Take time to reflect on the following questions and scripture reference.

- Why is it important to know your identity?
- What does being the *daughter* of the Most High Father mean?

Scripture to meditate on:

"My prayer is not for them alone. I pray also for those who will believe in me through their message, that all of them may be one, Father, just as you are in me and I am in you. May they also be in us so that the world may believe that you have sent me. I have given them the glory that you gave me, that they may be one as we are one: I in them and you in me. May they be brought to complete unity to let the world know that you sent me and have loved them even as you have loved me.

"Father, I want those you have given me to be with me where I am, and to see my glory, the glory you have given me because you loved me before the creation of the world. "Righteous Father, though the world does not know you, I know you, and they know that you have sent me. I have made you known to them, and will continue to make you known in order that the love you have for me may be in them and that I myself may be in them."

John 17:20-25

CHAPTER EIGHT

Marriage – Your Future Hope

Something within each of us desires to be wanted. To be called upon. To have someone rely upon us. We have all waited and wished for someone to just call or text and say, "Hi."

Or the feeling you get as you drive down the road and you see a couple holding hands and laughing together. There is something our Creator has placed in us that we desire to be held, attached, connected, and to know there is someone available anytime we need a hug. For those sisters who desire to have a husband, these are some of the qualities and interactions you should expect to share with him.

Someone with whom you can ask a question or share a concern or fear that you may have. Maybe it's an individual you can walk up to and wrap your arms around him from behind and catch him off guard. But once you wrap your arms around him, he knows your touch and doesn't fear. He starts laughing and smiling and holds on to your arms because he doesn't want you to let go. You want someone with whom you can share your fears and dreams without having any reservation regarding rejection. Yes! This is a person who you can trust to go up 13,000 feet in a plane to skydive and attach yourself to him with one parachute knowing he is the only one who can pull the cord to release the chute to save both of you. You can trust this individual. Praise God!

What does God say about this? Is there something wrong with me because I have these natural desires to be held, attached, loved, accepted, secure, and to be "naked" with someone, but it seems that every time I find someone on earth, I do it wrong or end up being so deeply hurt? That's very easy to do when we get all five senses, or may I say six senses involved. God made us to have all six senses for a reason. These six senses are sight, smell, sound, taste, touch, and the *sixth sense*, spiritual sensitivity. These six senses were not made to be stagnant, stale, or idle. God made them to be used in a healthy, whole, and unselfish manner within the boundaries that He knew were safe and yet stimulating.

Those boundaries as we have discussed throughout this book are only within the safety and sanctity of marriage. Let's do what I like to call going *back to the Garden* in Genesis chapter 2 and learn about a love story that puts *Romeo and Juliet* to shame. Now please take a moment to read verses seven through twenty-five, because I am going to dissect, break down, interpret, and comment on these verses based on what I believe the Holy Spirit has shown me.

So as you read, you can now see the Father and Creator of love knew that it was very important for Adam to get to know his reflection, Eve; and Eve was to know her reflection, Adam. This is what I call *Heaven on Earth*. There were no issues, concerns, or interruptions between Adam and Eve. No cell phones ringing, televisions playing loudly … "Who will be this year's winner of America's Got Talent?" or "Touchdown! What an amazing catch in the end zone!" There were no babies crying, or "Well, honey, I'm sorry, but I must go to work now." My point in sharing those examples is the importance of having undivided, one-on-one, intimate time with your spouse. Let's take a look at what Deuteronomy 24:5 says:

> *If a man has recently married, he must not be sent to war or have any other duty laid on him. For one year he is to be free to stay at home and bring happiness to the wife he has married.*
>
> (NIV)

Now let's begin reviewing what you read in Genesis 2:7-25, starting with verse seven. God formed Adam from the dust and breathed life into him. We are made in the image of God. Now in verse nineteen, you notice that God created the animals from the ground but did not breathe His life into them. They are not created in His image. Keep that in mind.

Look back to verses nine through fourteen. God provided everything Adam needed. First, He provided him with a place to live, the Garden of Eden. When the Father provides, He will meet your needs and your heart's desires. It had great-tasting fruit that was pleasing to all five of his natural physical senses (sight, smell, taste, sound, touch). It had a natural irrigation system from the rivers that watered the Garden. The first river mentioned is the only river that had a description that includes provision of gold, bdellium, and the onyx stone. One can assume, if the water that flows from the Garden is blessing the land outside the Garden, then it is likely bringing provision within the Garden.

Then God commissions Adam in verse fifteen with a job – tend to the Garden, cultivate it, and keep it nice and trim. Adam's primary responsibilities are to take care of the place that God provided for him to live, and enjoy the blessings that come with it. In sixteen and seventeen, God tells him that he may eat from every tree in the Garden except for the tree of the knowledge of good and evil, or he will die. Paraphrased, I believe that God is saying, "Now I am going to see if you will trust Me." Love is not just fully protecting someone, smothering them, or preventing them from getting hurt; but love is giving that person a free-will choice to trust in you. That is what God did for Adam; He put trust in Adam to choose life, the tree of life. Now, I'm going somewhere with this, Sister. Hang in there with me.

In verse eighteen, after God had provided for Adam a place to live, food to eat, and a task, He noticed that it was not good for man to be alone. It doesn't say that Adam mentioned to God, "Hey, Father, I am alone."

Nope. God knew that he was feeling alone. Our Creator knew that Adam needed someone with whom to enjoy, share, and experience all the blessings God had given him. First, God wanted to teach him something. In verses nineteen and twenty, He brings Adam the animals that God made and told him to name the animals. As Adam named the animals, he began to realize something . . . these living creatures were not made in the image of God. Not only that, they each had a reflection of the other. The male giraffe had a female giraffe, the male elephant had a female elephant, the male gorilla had a female gorilla, etc. Adam recognized that each one of these creatures were in pairs. Each male had a female counterpart. But for him, there was no match.

Look what King Solomon wrote in Ecclesiastes 4:7-12 about being alone:

Then I looked again at vanity under the sun. There was a certain man without a dependent, having neither a son nor a brother [I'll take the liberty to include "wife"], yet there was no end to all his labor. Indeed, his eyes were not satisfied with riches and he never asked, "And for whom am I laboring and depriving myself of pleasure?" This too is vanity and it is a grievous task. Two are better than one because they have a good return for their labor. For if either of them falls, the one will lift up his companion. But woe to the one who falls when there is not another to lift him up. Furthermore, if two lie down together, they keep warm, but how can one be warm alone? And if one can overpower him who is alone, two can resist him. A cord of three strands is not quickly torn apart.

Wow, the three-cord strand is going to be composed of you, your husband, and of course, Jesus, who is the center of your marriage. When you have the King who created the power of love within marriage as the glue, then your relationship will be strong enough to get through the attacks of the enemy. We witness from our successfully married Christian couples that marriage is work and worth every effort to keep.

Verse twenty-one explains that God began the first surgery in history to bring Adam his amazing partner of intimacy, Eve. The Surgeon of surgeons began His work. He gave Adam an all-natural anesthesia and put him to sleep. Then, He took a rib from his side and closed his wound up. By the way, I'm sure God in His perfection didn't leave a scar. But even if he did, scars can be perfect, too. If Adam had a scar, it would be a reminder of the blessing God gave him that was Eve.

To verse twenty-two, God took Adam's rib and formed, fashioned, perfected, built, and showed off His most beautiful being in the history of eternity, by creating Eve. Then the Creator woke up Adam and brought Eve to him, and Adam said, "Whoa, Man! I mean … I'll call her woman because that was my first expression when I saw the amazing creation my Father God had made for me!" All in good fun, but we know she was fashioned out of a man, as it is written in the Bible.

   I can imagine Adam began to sing a new song unto the Lord as he was pointing at his wife and said, "Look what the Lord has done! Look what the Lord has done! He made her body, right out of mine! He blessed me and right on time!"

In verse twenty-three, he called her *woman* because she was made by being taken out of him, a man. See, that's why when a woman gets married, she usually takes her husbands' last name. Verse twenty-four states that when a man leaves his father and mother he shall cleave unto his wife and become one flesh. Now the word *cleave* obviously has to do with being unified as one body but also goes beyond just the physical. I'd like to take a moment to break down the word *cleave*. I looked up the word cleave in *Merriam-Webster Dictionary* and it literally means *to adhere firmly and closely or loyally and unwaveringly*. Now, let's look at the definition of adhere. It states:

  1: to give support or maintain loyalty
  2: *obsolete*: accord
  3: to hold fast or stick by or as if by gluing, suction, grasping, or fusing
  4: to bind oneself to observance

Wow! Look at the second definition. It simply states the word *accord*, to which I found the following definitions:

transitive verb
1: to bring into agreement: reconcile
2: to grant or give especially as appropriate, due, or earned

intransitive verb
1 *archaic*: to arrive at an agreement

A Love Letter to the Ladies

2 *obsolete*: to give consent
3: to be consistent or in harmony; agree

In review, when a man cleaves to his wife, the following words define the behaviors and characteristics that a man should display to his wife: Give support, be loyal, bring into agreement, to grant or give as appropriate, due or earned, to be consistent or in harmony, to hold fast or stick by or as if by gluing, suction, grasping, or fusing; and last but certainly not the least, to bind oneself to observance.

What an amazing God! So in other words, to be *one flesh* or *one body*, unified. By the way, this is a reason you just can't rush through reading the Bible. Take your time and look very deeply at the meaning of specific words to get the full effect as we just did with the word *cleave*.

I also looked in *Strong's Concordance of the Bible* at the original Hebrew word of *cleave*. *Cleave* is linked to an Arabic word with its root meaning to cook or to be cooking. Just like cooking involves a mix of ingredients that sends off a wonderful smell and eventually tasty food that is enjoyed, sex is an action that involves all five senses. And, yes, our Creator meant sex in marriage to be hot and stimulating for both the man and woman. I will stop there, but it needed to be said.

In The Message version of the Bible, Paul states it appropriately in 1 Corinthians 7:1-5:

> *Now, getting down to the questions you asked in your letter to me. First, is it a good thing to have sexual relations? Certainly—but only within a certain context. It's good for a man to have a wife, and for a woman to have a husband. Sexual drives are strong, but marriage is strong enough to contain them and provide for a balanced and fulfilling sexual life in a world of*

sexual disorder. The marriage bed must be a place of mutuality—the husband seeking to satisfy his wife, the wife seeking to satisfy her husband. Marriage is not a place to "stand up for your rights." Marriage is a decision to serve the other, whether in bed or out. Abstaining from sex is permissible for a time if you both agree to it, and if it's for the purposes of prayer and fasting—but only for such times. Then come back together again. Satan has an ingenious way of tempting us when we least expect it.

And, last but certainly not least, verse twenty-five states:

And the man and his wife were both naked and were not ashamed.

This scripture means that they were physically nude and had not one drop of shame, concern, worry, or fear. They were comfortable walking around completely exposed in amazing scenery where they had never sinned or even known what sin was. Their Eros (erotic) love was uncompromised. Adam and Eve were pure virgins. They were *naked* physically, in their hearts (emotionally) and minds (mentally). They didn't have any memories of other people they saw nude because of poor choices of having premarital sex. They didn't have television or internet to voyeur (look at someone lustfully), and they didn't have romance novels or movies to pollute their mind. The only bodies that they ever saw was their own and each other's. Look at what 1 Corinthians 7:3-5 states:

The husband should fulfill his marital duty to his wife, and likewise the wife to her husband. The wife's body does not belong to her alone but also to her husband. In the same way, the husband's body does not belong to him alone but also to his wife. Do not deprive each other except by mutual consent and for a time, so that you may devote yourselves to prayer. Then come together again so that Satan will not tempt you because of your lack of self-control.

(NIV)

See, both Adam and Eve were able to have pure hearts and minds as they began to explore each other in absolute purity. One can imagine every time they expressed their love to one another, it felt fresh, clean, and new. They were without fear of comparing each other to their past sexual encounters and false expectations.

Wow! It is clear that the Creator's idea of sex and romance blows away the Hollywood version. There are no polluted flashbacks of past sexual experiences. No comparing past partners but simply pure experiences with each other.

Get ready, because as you begin to recommit yourself fully unto the Lord, He is going to honor you. You can begin brand new. You can be like a virgin all over again. Your past is your past, my dear sister. Remember what Jeremiah 29:11-13 states:

For I know the plans I have for you," says the Lord. "They are plans for good and not for disaster, to give you a future and a hope. In those days when you pray, I will listen. If you look for me wholeheartedly, you will find me.

(NLT)

Remember, my dear sister, as we discussed earlier, when you find your true intimacy in the Lord, that is how you find your true identity. You understand you belong to your Heavenly Father first. Now you can be led by your Father's hand to the man who is to be your husband. Praise His name for His promises, for His promises will come true in your life as you continue to put Him first. Remember, you are the daughter of the Most High Father. May His Spirit guide you into the promises that He has for you. Love ya, Sister!

This Prayer Is for You

One final thing. Since the title of this book is *A Love Letter to the Ladies*, we must give honor and glory to the King of hearts, the Lover of lovers and the One who created all kinds of love. Here is a love letter I wrote one day during my personal intimate prayer time with Him.

The Greatest Love that I can ever show You, God, is to spend alone time with You. My Lover and my Heart, please forgive me for all the times that I have put everything and everyone above You by making time for them and not You. I'm sorry for all of the distractions and the idols in my life. I repent now and throw them out of the door of my heart. I understand that You want to love me, and I want to love You. This goes beyond anything on Earth, beyond the intimacy of a husband and wife, beyond a virgin bride and virgin bridegroom who have been waiting and longing for many years to express themselves in a healthy and holy way by consummating their marriage with one another. Our love is beyond the love of an earthly father and mother who are witnessing and experiencing the birth of a child and finally holding the child in their arms for the first time. Our love is the love of our Heavenly Father who was willing to send His only begotten Son down from heaven unto Earth to suffer and die for our sins. Our love is this: "No greater love does a man have than this, to lay down his life for a friend!" That's what Your love is, Yeshua (Jesus)! My greatest love in return to You is to crucify my flesh with all its lusts and passions by spending quality time with You so You can mold me and make me to be in Your image, so I can reflect You and be like You! Then we can together share our love with others so they too can

A Love Letter to the Ladies

be joined as one with us! The mishpochah of our Abba! (The family of our Daddy)! Thank You, Jesus, for helping me break the selfishness in my life and not giving up on me, my Lover and my Friend. Thank You for Your love and patience with me and not divorcing me or disowning me like girlfriends and family members have! Your love makes me crazy for You and wants me to share it with others! Just like when a couple gets married and they drive in their car, announcing it to the world with the words "Just Married" painted on the windows and cans dragging behind. This is a much greater love, because it's Your unfailing love! May I continue to spend time with You, and may You continue to form me in Your beautiful image. May I have the honor with You to be by Your side as Your bride and lead many who are looking for love in all the wrong places and lead them to our wonderful love! Thank You Abba, thank You Yeshua and thank You, Comforter, for living inside me, in the part of my heart that is reserved only for You! You made my banquet ready, and Your banner over me is Your Love! Here I come, my Love! Here I am! Let's share our love with one another!

Chapter Eight: Reflections

Take time to reflect on the following questions and scripture references.

- Why did God say that it was not good for man to be alone?
- What does cleave mean, and also what is its true meaning of the Hebrew word found in Genesis 2:24?
- Be honest with yourself for a moment and ask yourself this question, "Am I a good candidate and ready to be a wife for one of my Heavenly Father's sons?"

Scriptures to mediate on:

An excellent wife, who can find? For her worth is far above jewels. The heart of her husband trusts in her, And he will have no lack of gain. She does him good and not evil All the days of her life.
Proverbs 31:10-12

He who did not spare his own Son, but gave him up for us all—how will he not also, along with him, graciously give us all things?
Romans 8:32 (NIV)

A Love Letter to the Ladies

Acknowledgments

    First, I would like to thank the Lover of lovers! The Lover of my soul who has a big billboard above me that states, "To the one I love more than he even knows or can comprehend!" The One I owe thanks to is my Eternal Father, my Eternal Brother, and my Eternal Comforting Spirit that lives in me! Hear, O'Israel, the Lord your God is One God! Thank You Adonai (Father), Yeshua (Jesus), and Ruach HaKodesh (Holy Spirit)! I owe Him all my thanks! He was patient with me when it took me nearly eight years to get back to writing this book.

    Second, I would like to thank all of my friends and spiritual family who never spoke death or defeat into me and challenged me to keep going to reach my goal in completing this manuscript. Thanks to my spiritual mother Marilyn for her loving patience with me and always showing me our loving Messiah through her constant example of Him. Thanks to Ira, Frank, Clarence, Rich, Jackie, Dominic, John, Greg, Alberta, Miriam, Michelle, Raushanah, Sherrelle, and many other friends. Also, I would like to mention my deepest gratitude and thanks to my friends Kristin and Kianna for your patience and time in assisting me by editing my book. But especially to my publisher and the one who spent many hours of time coaching me through my book, Julie Castro. To all of my rabbis and pastors who have personally spoken life into me, I give honor where honor is due and thank you from the bottom of my heart: Rabbis Harlon & Joyce Picker, Rabbi Cosmo Panzetta, Rabbi Allan Moorhead & Pastor Anita Moorhead, Pastor Gus Korkotselos and Pastors Reginald and Kelley Steele.

    Third, a heartfelt thanks to my biological family who contributed to this book. The truth is, if it wasn't for your being in my life, I would have never been challenged, encouraged, and yes, at times hurt. If I would have never experienced that hurt, I wouldn't be writing this book.

Fourth, I would like to give a special thanks to those who had a healthy influence on my life, especially my sisters Teresita and Star. Also, my sister Tina, who is waiting for me with Jesus in heaven—and what a reunion that is going to be! Star and Tina, thanks for showing me determination to live your lives to the best of your ability without having an earthly father present in your life and also for giving me a deep personal incentive to write this book, as if I were writing it for you. Also, thanks to my Grandma Theresa for doing her best to be a loving example while protecting me as much as I would be willing to heed to her warnings. Thanks to my uncle for expressing forgiveness and restoration to me. In addition, I send my thanks to my earthly father, Tanis. Thanks for your forgiveness when I asked. All is in the past, and I'm grateful to now have a healthy relationship with you. I am honored to carry the same name as you. A special thanks to my mama, Terri, who gave birth to me. Thanks for literally saving my life a couple of times. Thank you so much, Mom, for being the best mom you could be. I know you did your best as a single mother to raise me. I will always be your one and only son and firstborn child! Thanks for always doing your best to speak positive things into my life, always being someone who encouraged me to be my best, and making me feel like I was the best son in the world! Love ya, Mom!

Finally, this part may be weird to some of you, but I would like to thank myself. T.J., you learned how to encourage yourself in the Lord just like David did. Keep the self-motivation going and remember what your Heavenly Father told you, "Strive for a breath-by-breath intimate relationship with Me, Your Creator and Friend, and never put anyone or anything in the place of your heart that belongs only to Me! Also, love your neighbor/brother/sister, etc. as you love yourself. In other words, let others grow in Me without judging them, and do the same for yourself by being who you are in Me."

Notes

Chapter one: The Price of Purity

1. Taken from *Eyes Wide Open: Avoiding the Heartbreak of Emotional Promiscuity* by Brienne Murk. Copyright 2007 by Brienne Murk. Used by permission of Regal Books.

Chapter six: Where's My Rib!? Are You A Redeemed Rib?! (Heart Issues)

1. Taken from *The Five Love Languages: The Secret to Love That Lasts*, ©2010 by Gary D. Chapman. Used by permission of Northfield Publishing.www.5lovelanguages.com.

www.ingramcontent.com/pod-product-compliance
Lightning Source LLC
Chambersburg PA
CBHW050552300426
44112CB00013B/1890